THOMAS WOLFE

THOMAS WOLFE

THOMAS WOLFE

A Critical Study

BY

PAMELA HANSFORD JOHNSON

WILLIAM HEINEMANN LTD

LONDON　　　::　　　TORONTO

FIRST PUBLISHED 1947

PRINTED IN GREAT BRITAIN AT THE WINDMILL PRESS
KINGSWOOD, SURREY

CONTENTS

	PAGE
THE DOMESTIC CRITIC	1
THE STYLE	17
THE STORY OF EUGENE GANT	34
THE STORY OF GEORGE WEBBER	55
THE FOUR NOVELS	78
THE PHILOSOPHY	98
THE AMERICAN RICH	110
THE INCOMMUNICABLE PRISON	124
APPENDIX A	135
APPENDIX B	137

"La Renaissance élisabéthaine repand une odeur d'homme. Nous ne pouvons aujourd'hui la respirer sans vertige. C'est que nous sommes, pour ainsi dire, dépassionnés."

JEAN CASSOU

THE
DOMESTIC
CRITIC

THOMAS WOLFE died in the Johns Hopkins Hospital at Baltimore on September 15th, 1938, after an operation following upon pneumonia. The cause of his death was an acute cerebral infection. He was thirty-seven years old. He left behind him over a million words of unpublished manuscript.

He had worked all his life along the thread of his own experience, making monstrous variations upon the story of himself, had worked, not upon eight books, but upon one only; and not upon one vastly designed structure, as Proust's is designed, but back and forth, over the same ground again and again, elaborating, filling in, always with himself, either as Eugene Gant or as George Josiah Webber, for hero. Because the main narrative was fixed and unalterable, it mattered nothing to him at what point he took it up or let it lapse. If he felt like writing of one period in his life rather than of another, he would write Chapter 18 and follow it by Chapter 3, Chapter 4 and follow it by Chapter 50, throwing the finished section aside into the packing case that served him as desk and vault. From the mass of sketches, unrelated paragraphs, long stretches of story-telling, his posthumous books were pieced together.

Thomas Clayton Wolfe was born on October 3rd, 1900, in Asheville, North Carolina, the "Altamont, old Catawba", or "Libya Hill", of the novels. His father was

a stonecutter, a skilled artisan with a prodigious memory
for rhetorical poetry. "My father," Wolfe says in his
humble and beautiful account of his development as a
writer,

> ". . . . was a man with a great respect and veneration
> for literature. He had a tremendous memory, and he
> loved poetry, and the poetry that he loved best was
> naturally of the rhetorical kind that such a man would
> like. Nevertheless it was good poetry, Hamlet's
> Soliloquy, 'Macbeth', Mark Antony's Funeral Oration,
> Gray's 'Elegy', and all the rest of it. I heard it all as a
> child; I memorised and learned it all."

His mother was a boarding-house keeper. For Wolfe,
the seventh and by six years the youngest child of his
parents, there was little money to spare; but when he was
fifteen the family scraped up sufficient to send him to the
state university, where he edited the college magazine
and wrote one-act plays. One of these, *The Return of
Buck Gavin: the Tragedy of a Mountain Outlaw*, was staged
at the university with the author as leading man; later this
was printed in *Carolina Folk Plays* (second series, edited
by F. M. Koch, 1924), his first published work. The
success, modest enough, served to stiffen his belief in
himself, though he spoke about it dubiously and cynically
in a letter to Mrs. J. M. Roberts, who had been his teacher
in Asheville.

> "Professor Koch of Chapel Hill bounded into town
> a week or so ago, and looked me up. He wants to put
> one of my juvenile one-acts—the *Buck Gavin* thing—
> into his new book which Holt is bringing out soon.
> He is insistent, and has just sent me a copy of the thing.
> I'm not ashamed of the play, but I wrote it on a rainy
> night, when I was seventeen, in three hours. Some-

thing tells me I should hate to see my name attached now. Of course I couldn't tell Koch that.

"Besides, he had his chance two or three years ago, when he brought his first book out. Please, don't *publish*—but I'll give you my honest opinion: I believe his eagerness to publish the little play now comes from a suspicion that I'm going to get famous in a hurry now—God knows why!—and he wants to *ticket* me, so to speak. This is a rotten thing to say, but it's my honest opinion."*

It is more than probable that he did Professor Koch an injustice. Success was still a long way ahead.

In the summer of 1918 Wolfe worked as a checker on the Government docks at Newport News, Virginia, but two years later was at Harvard, studying dramaturgy under Professor Baker in the 47 Workshop. At this time he was obsessed by the idea of becoming a playwright, and he fired off his plays to the managements; but they all came back again. He wrote to Mrs. Roberts of the enthusiasm everyone seemed to feel about his plays, while nobody made any particular effort to produce them. One of the Appleton editors asked for Wolfe's play to read for publication. "I shall let him read it," wrote the proud young man of twenty-three, "I doubt that I shall let him publish—even if he wants to. Certainly, not so long as someone may produce it."

The Theatre Guild was cordial. Its officials wished to know him. They asked him to lunch. The play-reader mentioned him at the banquet of a dramatic association. The Provincetown Theatre kept his play for five months. Yet nothing happened.

"Everyone, you see, is enthusiastic, but I notice

* *Atlantic Monthly*, December, 1946.

that *I* earn my own living . . . But—I learn. I am acquiring patience. And I'm quite willing to wait a year or two for the unveiling exercises. Do you know, all that really matters right now is the knowledge that I am twenty-three, and a golden May is here.

"The feeling of immortality in youth is upon me. I am young, and I can never die. Don't tell me that I can. Wait until I'm thirty. Then I'll believe you."*

In 1924, still awaiting the unveiling exercises, he settled down to the wearying and seemingly thankless job of English instructor at Washington Square College, New York University. There is a fascinating serio-comic account of his work there, and of Abe Jones, the star student, in *Of Time and the River*. Between the first and second periods of instructorship he travelled abroad, and in the autumn of 1926 returned to London, where in a Chelsea rooming-house he began to write *Look Homeward Angel.*†

He worked frenetically, writing hour by hour in his big ledgers, lying sleepless in bed, then rising to switch on the light and read through what he had written during the day. He did not know what force had driven him to work, why he had come to London or why he stayed there. The phantasmagoric process of his life's effort had begun, time and the river were in flood.

"I actually felt that I had a great river thrusting for release inside of me, and that I had to find a channel into which its flood-like power could pour."

* From the *Atlantic Monthly*, December, 1946.

† This is according to Wolfe himself, in *The Story of a Novel*. Miss Aline Bernstein, however, says Wolfe told her that *Look Homeward Angel* was begun at Ilkley, and the outline finished there: he continued with the book when he went to London. It seems that the London rooming-house was not in Chelsea but in Horseferry Road, Westminster.

He returned to America, where he taught by day and wrote by night, completing the book in New York two and a half years after he had begun it.

When *Look Homeward Angel* was at last accepted by a publisher, he became conscious for the first time of "the awful, utter nakedness of print", the horror of the self-exposure that every writer must necessarily make. It was not simply the complex of the beginner: all through his life, whenever he had delivered a book into the publisher's hands, he would scheme to get it back again, to postpone the publication date in the hope that somehow or other, in some miraculous fashion, he might wrench it yet a little nearer to the unattainable ideal.

The world success of the book was scarred, for Wolfe, by its reception in his native town. It was a response he had not anticipated, although there was every reason why he might have done so. The fury of resentment was phenomenal. He was denounced from local pulpits and from street-corner meetings, subjected to the foulest anonymous abuse. One old lady whom he had known all his life wrote that though she had always been opposed to lynchings, she would not lift a finger to stop a mob dragging his "big, overgrown karkus across the public square".

Writers are often profoundly sensitive to the opinions of the community into which they were born; they are liable to be profoundly disturbed by 'what the neighbours think'. The boy from Altamont remembers that it was they who once gave him his orders, for they were the first adults to have control over his childhood. To him, Altamont is God and father, all-knowing, all-frustrating. Altamont, for its part, remembers him only in knee-pants, the child, the serf, the potential delinquent. Once upon a time it had only to order him down from an orchard wall and he jumped down, had only to threaten to tell his mother and he stopped chasing the fowls. It cannot tolerate the thought that he has cut free, is now no longer responsible to father, mother, schoolteacher or the disciplinary grocer at the corner shop. It has breathed the odour of man and grown giddy; it rounds upon the runaway in rancour and beaten pride.

"Altamont" believed itself pilloried, disgraced, and above all things found out; and despite the powerful autobiographical character of *Look Homeward Angel*, a character the author always, by a complex reasoning, violently disclaimed, Wolfe was stunned by the reaction. The fact that he did feel this sense of terror and amazement is comprehensible enough to any writer. The novelist is always far more innocent of malice than the neighbours think. He may use them as framework for his people; but once the new characters are elaborated, thickened in, they do become to him things of his own creation, emancipated from the originals. He inclines even to forget the originals altogether, because they have not, to him, played more than minor parts in the finished structures. "As far as my own book is concerned," Wolfe wrote, "I can truthfully say that I do not believe that there is a single page of it that is true to fact."

He felt that his people were not simply people of "Altamont", but of the whole continent of America. His work was far vaster than they, his intention far greater than any intention to examine closely small figures in a fenced landscape.

"I wrote about night and darkness in America, and the faces of the sleepers in ten thousand little towns;

and of the tides of sleep and how the rivers flowed forever in the darkness . . . I wrote about death and sleep, and of that enfeebled rock of life we call the city."

But this was highbrow stuff to Altamont, which didn't believe a word of it. The anger of his birth-town became one of the greatest inhibiting factors in Wolfe's career. In *The Prodigal's Return*, a sketch appearing in *The Hills Beyond*, he gives an impression, certainly a shadow beside the reality, of the misery it caused him, and in *You Can't Go Home Again* elaborates at length the theme of his reaction to the news from home.

The book had come at a time—

". . . when the better-known gentlemen and lady authors of the South were writing polished bits of whimsey about some dear Land of Far Cockaigne, or ironic little comedies about the gentle relics of the Old Tradition in the South, or fanciful bits about Negro mongrels along the Battery in Charleston . . . *Home to Our Mountains* was a novel that did not fit into any of these standardised patterns. It did not seem to have much pattern at all. The people of Libya Hill hardly knew what to make of it at first . . . For George Webber had used the scalpel in a way that that section of the country was not accustomed to. His book took the hide off the whole community; as a result of this it also took the hide off George Webber."

He—Thomas-George—received four main types of letter. The first was the usual anonymous abuse, sadic and obscene, arising less from any hurt caused by the author than from the cumulation of a hundred dark personal torments. The second was the plain, homespun threat: "We'll kill you if you ever come back here. You

[7]

know who." The third kind was reproachfully Christian, more repulsive than the first two in its gentle and pious brutality. It began, "My dear boy,"—continued: "You have crucified your family in a way that would make the agony of Christ upon the Cross seem light in the comparison. You have laid waste the lives of your kinsmen, and of dozens of your friends, and to us who loved you like our own you have driven a dagger to the heart, and twisted it, and left it fixed there where it must always stay."

Most nauseous of all, the letter from the man who believed that he and the novelist were wrapped cosily about in a like slime, like twin yolks in an egg:

". . . if I had known you were going to write this book, I could have told you lots of things. Why didn't you come to me? I know dirt about the people in this town you never dreamed of."

Miscellaneous letters accused him of "fouling his own nest", of being a "monster against life", of being "not Southern", and, fantastically, "not American."

The writers were entirely successful. They had meant to hurt: they had succeeded. Believing the author callous, they had rubbed in their reproach and abuse exceedingly hard, on the principle that it takes a big hammer to crack the skull of an ox. Had they but known it, the lightest touch of disapprobation would have had its effect at that particular time, when Thomas-George's nerves, frayed by hope and fear, monstrous ambitions and masochistic dreads, were quivering like antennæ.

In justice to Altamont there is this to be said: only public men and women ever come to realise just how private, in truth, they are. The private individual,

believing himself libelled, at once feels that the whole
world is laughing at him, as well it may be, for his village
is his world, and his neighbours are to him, in his day-
to-day life, the whole of mankind. Also, he does not
appreciate the shortness of memory. It seems to him
that he is pilloried forever, with the eyes of the crowd
forever upon his face; when, in fact, if he has the patience
to endure for less than nine days, he will see the crowd's
attention distracted by the first dog-fight or football
match. Thomas-George did cause great misery to his
family and to many of his friends. That their misery
might be considered a small thing to sacrifice to the
making of a masterpiece was not a consideration one
could reasonably expect to appeal, or even to occur, to
them. The only test of "rights and wrongs" lay in the
future. Who would in the end be the more repentant?
The libeller of Altamont, or the Altamont critic? Quite
certainly, despite the bitterness of his experience, it was
not Thomas-George, who was ultimately in no doubt
whatsoever as to the value of his own work.

The book's reception by the professional critics
exceeded the author's greatest hopes. There is a touching
and humorous account of his tentative approach to his
reviews.

"Whenever a notice of his work appeared in one of
the best magazines or weekly journals, he could hardly
bring himself to read it; neither could he go away
from it and leave it unread. He would approach it as a
man creeps stealthily to pick a snake up by the tail,
his heart leaping at the sight of his name. He would
scan the last line first, then with a rush of blood to his
face he would plunge into it at once, devouring the
whole of it as quickly as he could. And if he saw that

it was going to be 'good', a feeling of such powerful joy and exultancy would well up in his throat that he would want to shout his triumph from the windows. If he saw that the verdict was going to be 'thumbs down', he would read on with agonised fascination, and his despair would be so great that he would feel he was done for, that he had been exposed to the world as a fool and a failure, and that he would never be able to write another line."

After the New York praise his mail began to change in character. The flood of damning letters continued, but with them came messages of praise from complete strangers, invitations to lunch, dinner and tea: and the telephone rang all day.

All of this soothed and consoled; but it never cured. Wolfe's Achilles heel was this—the passion for being liked and, conversely, the dread of being hated. The wound it received gave him the title for his last and (so far as it reveals the author) most important book: *You Can't Go Home Again*.

The letters to Mrs. Roberts contain a curious side-light upon the whole business of the "Asheville libel". Wolfe, like many intensely kind people, could be startlingly insensitive to the feelings of others: but insensitive less from intent than from an automatic shutting-off of certain parts of the mind. He wrote to Mrs. Roberts of a projected novel, which was to be called *Passage to England* and which, it seems, would have contained two incidents that later appeared in *Of Time and the River*. He proposed to send Mrs. Roberts the prologue, together with other manuscripts: she was to act as his censor and to despatch what she thought suitable to the local paper, *The Citizen*, with the proviso that in no circumstances was it to be published under Wolfe's name.

"We are children—we must have an audience: and if my audience may be the people of a little North Carolina town, well and good. That is my whole desire for the present . . ."
He continues:

"I appoint you my censor: I have not been careful of myself in what I have said or am going to say—careful, that is, of what the townsfolk may think. That would be too petty, too dishonest. You must not be careful of that either in going over the manuscripts—it is not at all important. I think the sole thing—the *principal* thing—is the relation any of it may have to my family, to their position in the community. I shall never be too 'advanced' to respect that."*

This was in March, 1925, when the realities of a publishing day seemed a long way ahead. Four years later, by the time *Look Homeward Angel* was completed, Wolfe was writing to Mrs. Roberts in a different fashion.

"I hope you may be wrong in thinking what I have written may distress members of my family, or anyone else. Certainly, I would do anything to avoid causing anyone pain—except to destroy the fundamental substance of my book. I am afraid, however, that if anyone is distressed by what seemed to me a very simple and unoffending story, their feeling when the book comes out will be much stronger. And the thought of that distresses *me* more than I can tell you."†

He had been warned. Mrs. Roberts had warned him what to expect, and he dreaded it; yet he was determined

* *Atlantic Monthly*, December, 1946.

† *Atlantic Monthly*, January, 1947.

now that the book should be published as it stood. He argued energetically in advance against the wrath to come:

"I can only assure you that my book is a work of fiction, and that no person, act, or event has been deliberately and consciously described . . . Dr. Johnson said a man would turn over half a library to make a single book; so may a novelist turn over half a town to make a single figure in his novel . . . The world a writer creates is his own world—but it is moulded out of the fabric of life, what he has known and felt—in short, out of himself. How in God's name can it be otherwise?"*

Time, however, tends to soften the queasy conscience, especially if the consequences of the fault committed come tardily. Wolfe forgot his scruples; nothing mattered to him but the book itself. By now the people in it had become to him neither creatures of his own creation, nor persons translated out of life on to the page: but people with an independent being and right of their own, living in "a land more kind" (and more cruel) "than home, more large than earth," which was yet the America of his own possessing.

When the anticipated storm broke, it was not the right kind of storm, not the kind he had imagined that it would be. It was a storm for which he was utterly unprepared, against which his defence measures prepared in advance seemed useless, and in which he found himself naked. He had known it would come; he had expected it. And yet it took him by complete surprise.

This, the shock delivered by the Asheville critic, was the most serious inhibiting factor of his life, leaving a sore upon his mind that it was agony to touch. If he

* *Atlantic Monthly*, January, 1947.

touched upon it himself, again and again, this was rather upon the principle that if we have an aching tooth it gives us grim satisfaction to joggle it and so treble the agony. A second factor, however, was his own success. He began to feel, not only guilt, but the dead weight of responsibility. He had been so much praised: so much was expected of him. Was his first book simply a flash in the pan? Could he hope to justify the mountain of belief that had risen up behind him?

The long pause between the publication of *Look Homeward Angel* and *Of Time and the River* was filled with the frantic reaping of material, material that seemed to stretch away for a million light-years; was filled with the experiences of travel; was filled with doubt, anguished self-searching and the nightmare labour of selection from riches that were all too vast.

"I am not even a skilled writer . . . It is for just this reason, because I blunder, because every energy of my life and talent is still involved in this process of discovery, that I am speaking as I speak here."

Ominously, he had begun to have an absorbing doubt that he might not live long enough to complete his work; and with this doubt came the obsession of Guilt and Time.

"I had been long enough from home—I had grown old in some evil and enchanted place, I had allowed my life to waste and rot in the slothful and degrading surfeits of Circean time."

To his home, friends, people, he now felt a forsaken trust. For over five years the uncertainty, the fear, the despair continued; the stacks of manuscript mounted up. He had planned to call the new book *The October Fair*. He had, at the urging of his editor, cut it again and again, but it was still about twice the length of *War and Peace*.

Then two things happened. The first was a sudden acceptance that his life was going to be always as it was now, that the struggle and frustration would never end.

"One bright cell in the brain or heart or memory would now blaze on forever . . . I knew at last I had become a writer: I knew at last what happens to a man who makes the writer's life his own."

It is as well that the acceptance was made at this point. Time was already running short.

The second thing was this. His editor told him that, whether he liked it or not, the book was finished, and that Wolfe's job now was to begin sorting the accumulated manuscript. This editor, Maxwell Perkins of Scribner, a man whose service to Wolfe's work it is impossible to over-estimate, suggested that the mass of writing fell naturally into two cyclic movements. Together they drove the first part into shape, and in 1936 it was published under the title, *Of Time and the River*.

Wolfe felt he could not bear to stay in America for the publication, so he returned to Paris. There he received Perkins' cable telling him that the book had been magnificently praised, although there had been some criticism where it might have been expected. Wolfe was first elated, then cast down into the pit. He feared and he fretted, wondering whether Perkins had perhaps meant to tell him, delicately, that the book had been a failure after all. The more he looked at the cable, the more certain he felt that this was indeed so. He knew no ease until he had wired back to America for reassurance, and had received it.

Wolfe, in fact, had no sort of hide.* A man of gigantic stature (his height was six foot six) his sensitivity was extreme. He wrote to match his height, he roared to match it, he ate and drank to match it; but among the Lilliputians of Altamont he was a feeble Gulliver. Their miniature arrows had found their mark and sunk their poison.

Shortly before his death he wrote to Edward Aswell of Harper, now his publisher,† that he was turning aside from "lyrical and identifiable personal autobiography. He now sought, and hoped now to obtain, through free creation, a release of his inventive power which the more shackling limitations of identifiable autobiography did not permit."‡ In short, he was prepared to drop the hero Eugene Gant, so sharp a reminder of his own vulnerability, and become George Webber.

He felt himself still the voice of emerging America, the expression of a new and rootless culture. It was the task of the American writer to draw new traditions out of himself and his experience, and from

". . . the enormous space and energy of American life . . . Out of the billion forms of America, out of the savage violence and the dense complexity of all its swarming life; from the unique and single substance of this land and life of ours, must we draw the power and energy of our own life, the articulation of our speech, the substance of our art."

* "My state is not bad—in spite of the fact that I am considered arrogant and proud (the protective coloration of one who was born without his proper allowance of hide)." *Letter to Mrs. J. M. Roberts* (*Atlantic Monthly*, January, 1947).

† See Appendix A.

‡ Edward Aswell, "Note on Thomas Wolfe" appended to *The Hills Beyond*.

At his death two long novels had been published (*Look Homeward Angel*, 1929, *Of Time and the River*, 1936), one short novel (*A Portrait of Bascom Hawke*, 1932), a longish tale (*The Web of Earth*, 1932), one book of sketches that cannot properly be called short stories (*From Death to Morning*, 1935) and the remarkable essay, *The Story of a Novel*, 1936. After he died the three posthumous books were edited, and published in America. They are *The Web and the Rock* (1939), *You Can't Go Home Again* (1940)—this is the second part of the George Webber chronicle—and *The Hills Beyond*, reprinted in 1941 with a "Note on Thomas Wolfe" by Edward C. Aswell. *The Web and the Rock*, with foreword by J. B. Priestley, has been published in England this year (1947).

THE STYLE

In the style of Wolfe is his essence. It is for this that we read him—not for narrative, not for philosophy, not for the desire to study more intently the nature of human thought and behaviour. The narrative is dictated by the circumstances of his own life, and runs wild as an unsheared hedge. The philosophy is half-baked—a sequence of ideas held to-day because of yesterday's impressions, and just as likely to be altered to-morrow. His observation of the ways of man refreshes and stimulates the memory: we think—yes, this was so, this is how it was, this is the proper cause of that resulting action: but we are not constantly amazed by revelation, as we are amazed by the discoveries of Joyce, or Virginia Woolf, or Proust.

We read Wolfe primarily for his rhetorical poetry, which he delivers from his great height with the authority of a prophet who has seen the clouds open to reveal a calligraphy of fire upon the white spaces of the air.

To him all things are marvellous. He never learned the sophistication that brings fear of an audience. He never doubted his own vision, never paused to think—"Yes, this all seems very marvellous to me, but these older and wiser persons sitting around—are they likely to smile at me because the things that fill me with wonder are things at which they wondered only in their youth, and have now set aside with all the other commonplace marvels of human experience?"

"Then the moon blazed down upon the vast desolation of the American coasts, and on all the glut and hiss of tides, on all the surge and foaming slide of waters on lone beaches. The moon blazed down on eighteen thousand miles of coast, on the million sucks and scoops and hollows of the shore, and on the great wink of the sea, that are the earth minutely and eternally. The moon blazed down upon the wilderness, it fell on sleeping woods, it dripped through moving leaves, it swarmed in weaving patterns on the earth, and it filled the cat's still eye with blazing yellow. The moon slipt over mountains and lay like silence in the desert, and it carved the shadows of great rocks like time. The moon was mixed with flowing rivers, and it was buried in the heart of lakes, and it trembled on the water like bright fish. The moon steeped all the earth in its living and unearthly substance, it had a thousand visages, it painted continental space with ghostly light; and its light was proper to the nature of all the things it touched: it came in with the sea, it flowed with the rivers, and it was still and living on clear spaces in the forest where no men watched."

This is the very satisfaction of our outward-looking, of our desire to stand upon the highest peak of the world and see at a glance all its rivers and forests and seas, its nights and its mornings, its thrones, dominations and powers. It gathers up a vast space and shrinks it into the scope of vision. To look down from Wolfe's Sinai is to look down upon the relief map of a continent, with cupfuls of water for the sea and spoonfuls for the lakes: and to become a giant.

Wolfe's feeling for the colour, the music and the shape of words is extraordinary; there is no American writer to whom language in itself means so much. He couples for onomatopœic effect words not strictly onomatopœic in themselves, but having that significance for him. For example, "the glut and hiss of tides." "Hiss" is an onomatopœic word, "glut" is not; but "glut", for Wolfe, had the slap and suck of a heavy driving wave, and is here a word of sound. And again—"the million sucks and scoops and hollows of the shore." All these three nouns Wolfe has *heard*. What he sees is not the static image of sands scooped out by the sea, but the sea itself actually in the process of sculpting them. By infusing the idea of sound into these visual words, he has telescoped the process of days and years into an action that we can watch in moments. His prose reduces to our immediate comprehension not only the spaces of the world, but also its eternal evolution.

"Who owns the earth? Did we want the earth that we should wander on it? Did we need the earth that we were never still upon it? Whoever needs the earth shall have the earth: he shall be still upon it, he shall rest within a little space, he shall dwell in one small room forever."

Wolfe prefaces each one of his novels with a prose-poem, and poetry is mingled as inextricably with the body of his work as it is with the narrative of the Old Testament. The style of it derives, indeed, from the poetic books of the Bible and is influenced also, so far as rhythm and sonority are concerned, by Whitman. In its very distinctiveness, in the grandiose flow, the rhetoric, the choice of the harsh, the round and glowing word, the startling image, it is fair game for the parodist and the imitator; but the force that is in it, a force freed by Wolfe's intense desire to achieve on paper the highest possible expression of the grandeur he saw upon earth, is inimitable, and beyond mockery.

"Could I make tongue say more than tongue could utter! Could I make brain grasp more than brain could think! Could I weave into immortal denseness some small brede of words, pluck out of sunken depths the roots of living, some hundred thousand magic words that were as great as all my hunger, and hurl the sum of all my living out upon three hundred pages!"

The words strike response from the heart as the sun strikes arrows of bronze from the shield. In their clangour, their gasping weight of effort, they force the imagination to the realisation of Wolfe's whole being and desire as narrowly, as nearly, as the battering-ram breaches the walls that will not quite yield. It is the effort of Hotspur, whom the lines remember:

"By heaven, methinks it were an easy leap
To pluck bright honour from the pale-faced moon;
Or dive into the bottom of the deep
Where fathom-line could never touch the ground,
And pluck up drowned honour by the locks."

Wolfe's words: pluck, sunken, depths, roots, hurl. Hotspur's: leap, pluck, dive, deep, drowned, locks. All these words imply descent into the mind to bring up the drowned Idea.

Wolfe writes vast, cumbrous passages of monumental beauty, prose-poems as wild, as disturbing as anything in America's literature. When he speaks of Loss—"O lost and by the wind grieved, ghost come back again!"—he speaks not merely of his own loss, but of some lost secret for which the millions of America are forever in milling search . . . "Of wandering for ever and the earth again . . . of seedtime, bloom, and the mellow-dropping harvest. And of the big flowers, the rich flowers, the strange, unknown flowers . . . Who owns the earth? Did we want the earth that we should wander on it? Did we need the earth that we were never still upon it?"

Strangest and most evocative poem of all is this prophecy, which occurs in the final paragraph of the final book, concluding the "Letter to Foxhall Edwards:"

"Something has spoken to me in the night, burning the tapers of the waning year; something has spoken in the night, and told me I shall die, I know not where. Saying:

" 'To lose the earth you know, for greater knowing; to lose the life you have, for greater life; to leave the friends you love, for greater loving; to find a land more kind than home, more large than earth—

" 'Whereon the pillars of this earth are founded, towards which the conscience of the world is tending— a wind is rising, and the rivers flow.' "

This is instantly moving because of its "supernatural" quality. Whatever it was that inspired the statement, it has upon it the command and hush of prophecy. Yet it is not a statement that flowed straight from the mind to the paper; it is most exquisitely and curiously formed. It is interesting to notice the dominant shapes that appear in Wolfe's image. First there are the converging rivers and then, rising above them, the uprights: the tapers of the year, the pillars of the earth. In a shadowy fashion, these shapes give to this passage the visual quality so pronounced in the whole of Wolfe's work.

The passage opens with an announcement, twice repeated, of the revelation of the author's imminent death. This is followed by a poem, beautiful and formal in design (three pentameters, one hexameter, three pentameters) which expresses the idea of joy and fulfilment beyond death. The words used are very simple, in Wolfe's New Testament, and not Old Testament mood: "earth," "land," "life," "friends," "home," "pillars," "conscience," "rivers." The poem summarises the desire from which his life's work springs, the desire for homecoming, and is one of the most flawless conclusions to any novel in the English language.

Wolfe's poetry derives from Whitman the unexpected image, the positive statement, the towering authority; but is fundamentally divorced from the philosophy.

> "I believe a leaf of grass is no less than the journey
>   work of the stars,
> And the pismire is equally perfect, and a grain of sand,
>   and the egg of the wren,
> And the tree-toad is a chef-d'œuvre for the highest,
> And the running blackberry would adorn the parlours
>   of heaven,
> And the narrowest hinge in my hand puts to scorn
>   all machinery,
> And the cow crunching with depressed head sur-
>   passes any statue,
> And a mouse is miracle enough to stagger sextillions
>   of infidels."

The images of the adorning blackberry, the hinge of the hand, the sextillions of infidels, would have been possible to Wolfe, and so would the pairing and contrasting of the nature-words and man-words:

tree-toad   )   blackberry)   hand   )   cow
chef d'œuvre)   parlours)   machinery)   statue

but the thorough-going Brahma-philosophy would not. Wolfe did not believe that in himself he was all things: he believed that he himself, as a man, was higher than all things.

He was, however, as capable as Whitman of the sudden descent from the sublime to the ridiculous.

> "I find I incorporate gneiss, coal, long-threaded moss, fruits, grain, esculent roots,
> And am stucco'd with quadrupeds and birds all over,
> And have distanced what is behind me for good reasons,
> But call anything back again when I desire it."

Wolfe, if he could not imagine himself stuccoed with quadrupeds and birds, could break without much warning into this kind of thing:

> "'Oh, you big, dumb, beautiful Boston bitch,' he panted amorously, 'just turn your face to me—and look at me—and by God! I will! I will! . . . By God, I'll do it!—Oh, you sweet, dumb, lovely trollop of a Back Bay—Ann!' he cried exultantly. 'Oh, by God, I'll thaw you out, I'll melt your ice, my girl!'"

And later:

> "'Oh, Ann! . . . You lovely bitch! You big, dark, dumb, lovely, sullen Boston bitch! . . . Oh, you bitch! You bitch!' he groaned, and seizing her hand, he caught it to him and said desperately, 'Ann, Ann, I love you! You're the greatest . . . grandest . . . best . . . most beautiful girl that ever lived . . . Ann! Look at me—you big, ox-dumb brute. . . .'"

With the dialogue of physical passion Wolfe is ever uneasy, and he takes refuge in a kind of voluptuous rowdyism.

The dialogue of ordinary human intercourse, however, he achieves with the ease that arises from an ear perfectly attuned to the shorthand of daily speech, the serviceable omission, the preservation of breath by the labour-saving glance or shrug.

His mother and his sister Helen are seeing the young Eugene off on the train that will take him to the University. Eliza, sad, nagging, an inveterate hinter, is talking to her soured daughter, who is dully and childlessly married, bitter, illumined only by her own coarse, warm, desperate humour. They have been speaking of some friend who bore her baby at the age of forty-four. Helen says, with her air of "rough banter" and a look full of sadness, that in this case there may yet be a chance for her.

" 'Chance!' the mother cried strongly, with a little scornful pucker of the lips—'why, of course there is! If I was your age again I'd have a dozen—and never think a thing of it.' For a moment she was silent, pursing her reflective lips. Suddenly a faint sly smile began to flicker at the edges of her lips, and turning to the boy, she addressed him with an air of sly and bantering mystery:

" 'Now, boy,' she said—'there's lots of things that you don't know . . . you always thought you were the last—the youngest—didn't you?'

" 'Well, wasn't I?' he said.

" 'H'm!' she said with a little scornful smile and an air of great mystery—'There's lots that I could tell you——'

" 'Oh, my God!' he groaned, turning towards his sister with an imploring face. 'More mysteries! . . . The next thing I'll find that there were five sets of triplets after I was born—Well, come on, Mama,' he cried impatiently. 'Don't hint around all day about it . . . What's the secret now—how many were there?'

" 'H'm!' she said with a little bantering, scornful, and significant smile.

" 'O Lord!' he groaned again—'Did she ever tell you what it was?' Again he turned imploringly to his sister.

"She snickered hoarsely, a strange high-husky and derisive falsetto laugh, at the same time prodding him stiffly in the ribs with her big fingers:

" 'Hi, hi, hi, hi, hi,' she laughed. 'More spooky business, hey? You don't know the half of it. She'll be telling you next you were only the fourteenth.'

" 'H'm!' the older woman said, with a little scornful smile of her pursed lips. 'Now I could tell him more than that! The fourteenth! Pshaw!' she said contemptuously—'I could tell him——'

" 'O God!' he groaned miserably. 'I knew it! . . . I don't want to hear it.'

" 'K, k, k, k, k,' the younger woman sniggered derisively, prodding him in the ribs again.''

This is all perfectly realistic, accurately heard and recorded. The sister's interjections—'hi, hi, hi,' 'k, k, k, k,' have more derisive an effect than any which could be made by words, by comment, or by the routine laughter-symbols. The stammer of Eugene's brother Luke is reproduced with the same economy, the same sparing of the eye that might be troubled by too many small dashes on the printed page.

It may be noted, from this passage, how Wolfe employed the repetition of certain words to force a mood into the reader's mind. "Banter" is used three times, "sly" twice, "scornful" three times, "imploring" twice, "groaned" three times. It is a curious and deliberate trick of emphasis, extraordinarily effective and sometimes cinematic. The attention is concentrated upon Eliza's face as if it were shown in close-up. Her lips "pucker", are "reflective", a "faint, sly smile" flickers at their edges, they are scornfully "pursed". The repetition of the word "lips" four times in the passage quoted does not seem redundant, but instead gives the effect of an intense visual clarity.

Wolfe acknowledged a debt to James Joyce, who, he claimed, had exerted a powerful influence upon his work. This would seem less obvious to the reader. Certain passages in the first two novels show an attempt at the stream-of-consciousness method, but they are few and brief, and the method is nowhere applied in Joyce's fluid and unbroken fashion. Wolfe copies Joyce on these rare occasions with a rather irritating devotion and skill; but it is no native form of expression, and these rare passages are out of tone with the body of his work and never merge into it. Wolfe's purely narrative sections are written objectively, directly, and with clarity.

Esther Jack is giving her grand party. As a treat for her guests she has invited the latest "craze"—Piggy Logan, who, with his puppet show, is now regarded as an artist more significant than Leonardo da Vinci.

"The chemises of such inflated personalities as Goethe, Ibsen, Byron, Tolstoy, Whitman, Dickens, and Balzac, had been ruthlessly investigated by some of the most fearless intellects of the day and found to be largely filled with straw wadding. Almost everything and everybody was in the process of being debunked—except the debunkers, and Mr. Piggy Logan and his dolls."

In his professional costume, his turtle-necked sweater,

canvas trousers, tennis shoes, knee-pads and football
helmet, he crouches in the Jack salon before a gilded
crowd and manipulates his toys. He has brought with
him, to gate-crash the party, a crowd of ill-mannered,
strained and neurotically bright young people, upon
whom he can rely for admiration: upon this occasion
their presence is not altogether unnecessary, for Mrs.
Jack's invited guests are already beginning to know that
slight staling which comes to festivities when most of
the food has been eaten and most of the best jokes have
been made.

"There were a good many acts of one kind or
another, and at last the trapeze performers were brought
on. It took a little while to get this act going because
Mr. Logan, with his punctilious fidelity to reality,
had first to string up a little net below the trapezes.
And when the act did begin it was unconscionably
long, chiefly because Mr. Logan was not able to make
it work. He set the little wire figures to swinging
and dangling from their perches. This part went all
right. Then he tried to make one little figure leave its
trapeze, swing through the air, and catch another
figure by its downswept hands. This wouldn't work.
Again and again the little wire figure soared through
the air, caught at the outstretched hands of the other
doll—and missed ingloriously. It became painful.
People craned their necks and looked embarrassed.
But Mr. Logan was not embarrassed. He giggled
happily with each new failure and tried again. It
went on and on. Twenty minutes must have passed
while Mr. Logan repeated his attempts. But nothing
happened. At length, when it became obvious that
nothing was going to happen, Mr. Logan settled the

whole matter himself by taking one little figure firmly between two fat fingers, conveying it to the other, and carefully hooking it on to the other's arms. Then he looked up at his audience and giggled cheerfully, to be greeted after a puzzled pause by perfunctory applause."

It is simple and funny, and the effect is achieved without emphasis. Indeed, Wolfe's dialogue and narrative *is* unemphatic and straightforward save when there is some special effect to be made: and the passages of poetry are thereby thrown into a stronger relief. Yet they are never separated from the main body of the story, but grow as naturally out of it as shoots from the trunk of a tree, firmly-rooted, and of a kind with it. No modern Lamb could edit a *Tales from Wolfe* by the method of plucking out the poetry; any such attempt would leave an incoherence and a bleeding.

It must be remembered that, with the exception of *Look Homeward Angel*, Wolfe's novels were not planned and built as a whole, but are the selected products of a vast mass of more or less heterogeneous material. The train journey from Altamont to New York in *Of Time and the River* occupies sixty-two pages of close print in the Heinemann edition; in its original form it was the length of an entire novel. It is therefore unlikely that Wolfe was able to achieve a great deal of textual revision. The poetic passages are obviously the result of great concentration, but narrative and dialogue sweep along in a torrent, and there are slacknesses to be found in them. Wolfe is a stylist where Dreiser is not; but, like Dreiser, he does not consider himself bound by the orthodoxies of English composition. Conjunctions and prepositions fall as they will; the author is striving for the maximum force of expression, and not the maximum of elegance.

"They got out of the car. Joel took his valise, and like a person walking in a dream, he followed him across the porch, into a large and dimly lit entrance-hall. Joel put his valise down in the hall, and turning, whispered . . ."

This passage, with its repetitions and ambiguities, shows Wolfe's casual routine fashion of crossing the space between one important incident and another. It is preceded by a long complex sentence of great visual beauty:

"It was a dream-house, a house such as one sees only in a dream—the moonlight slept upon its soaring wings, its white purity, and gave the whole enormous structure an aerial delicacy, a fragile loveliness like some enchanted structure that one sees in dreams . . ."

—and is followed by the description of Eugene's entry into the Pierce mansion:

"He nodded, unable to speak, and in silence followed his guide down the hall and through the house. Joel opened a door: the blazing moonlight fell upon the vast, swarded lawn and sleeping woods of that magic domain known as Far Field Farm. And that haunting and unearthly radiance fell as well upon the white wings of that magic house and on a group of its fortunate inhabitants who were sitting on the terrace.

"The two young men went out: forms rose to greet them."

The connecting link between these two passages is so perfunctory as to cause a momentary break in mood, and there are flaws of a similar kind throughout Wolfe's entire work.

There are lapses, too, of a more positive nature than this, probably the result of passing at too great a speed over transitional sections.

"The fellows . . . grew up to be hoboes, pool-room loafers, pimps and bullies living off a whore."

Only one whore to this intolerable deal of fellows? But this is not the kind of inexactitude that would have worried Wolfe in his own writing or in the writing of anyone else. The end, the total cumulative effect, was everything; any detail that contributed to it was therefore right for its own sake and in being accepted was justified.

His appetite for the rich, for the strange, for the gorgeous was Elizabethan: he would have been capable as Webster of conceiving a duke walking at midnight in a lane behind St. Mark's Church, bearing the leg of a man upon his shoulder. What was drab, rotten and foul he invested with a gorgeousness of his own.

"Aye! to call me forth from coolness and the gladed sweetness of cool grass to sweat my way through Niggertown in the dream torpor of the afternoon: to sweat my way up and down that grassless, treeless horror of baked clay; to draw my breath in stench and sourness, breathe in the funky nigger stench, sour wash-pots and branch-sewage, nigger privies and the sour shambles of the nigger shacks; to sear my sight and soul with little snot-nosed nigger children fouled with dung, and so bowed out with rickets that their little legs look like twin sausages of fat, soft rubber; so to hunt, and knock at shack-door, so to wheedle, persuade, and cajole, in order to find some other sullen wench to come and sweat her fourteen hours a day for seven days a week—and for three dollars!"

This picture of the negro quarter of Libya Hill, seen through the eyes of a boy forced from his play to run messages for an abominated and unimaginative aunt, is painted with savagery; yet an element of pleasure is in it. Wolfe does not hate what he is able to turn into richness, whether it is filth, or cruelty, or death: his contempt is always for what is withered and mean. Libya Hill's halcyon glades and her negro quarter were both part of his life, complementary each to each; without knowing the one, he could not have known the other. His real anger and despite is expressed in a different fashion.

At the end of the Young Faustus section in *Of Time and the River* is an incident which illustrates Wolfe's detestation of a cruelty that may in no way be endowed with richness, as it is a poor and avaricious thing in itself. Eugene and Starwick are out for a walk one spring morning. Starwick, elegant, insouciant, is harmlessly showing off his mastery over a small and frisking dog. The young men come suddenly face to face with old acquaintances, Edward Horton and his wife Effie, cheerful, back-slapping philistines who, under their friendly banter, conceal an ugly enviousness and a frenzied desire to hurt.

" 'And here is *Mister* Starwick!' Effie now cried brightly. '—And I *wish* you'd *look!*' she went on, as if enraptured by the spectacle—'all dressed up with a walking-stick and a dog—and yes, *sir!*' she exclaimed ecstatically, after an astonished examination of Frank's sartorial splendour—'wearing a bee-yew-teeful brown tweed suit that looks as if it just came out of the shop of a London tailor! . . . *My! my! my!* . . . I tell *you!*' she went on admiringly—'I just wish the folks back home could see us now, Pooly——' "

Under this veiled attack, which is now launched alternately by husband and wife, Starwick grows quieter and quieter, saying only "Quite", or "Ace"—the monosyllable that serves him for Yes—or calling peremptorily to the dog.

"He snapped his fingers and the little dog came trotting meekly towards him. Before Starwick's cold and scornful impassivity, Effie's broad and wholesome face did not alter a jot from its expression of radiant goodwill, but suddenly her eyes, which, set in her robust and friendly countenance, were the tortured mirror of her jealous, envious, possessive and ravenously curious spirit, had grown hard and ugly, and the undernote of malice in her gay tones was more apparent than ever when she spoke again."

The whole incident, which is related without elaboration, is full of harshness and pain, the drill close to the nerve. Though Wolfe's charity is later extended to the Hortons, he is quite unable to enrich them by it. In contrast with his feeling towards this couple, his feeling towards the negro quarter, with its unspeakable drowsy squalor, is warm with love.

To Wolfe, richness is all. He loads every rift with ore until, at times, the whole work comes dangerously near to cracking under the strain. Life is to him so lavish of wealth that he is forever straining to repay the debt with the currency of language. A greater "taste", as we accept this proud and finical word, would have saved him from the cannibalistic love-scenes with Esther, the abusive apostrophising of Ann, the bellows, the howls, the fist-clenchings, the bursts of rolling and windy verbosity; but had he possessed it, he would have been infinitely less the man and less the genius. He had sufficient confidence not to care for the scribbled stricture in the margin, the pencilled underlining and exclamation-mark, the little smiling deprecation, the quibble of the critic "European and Fancy"; his very faultiness is a part of his power, and this he realised, and of this made a matter for pride. It is significant that he was really angry with the reviewer who wrote of his "barbaric yawp".

The trouble with much of our own writing to-day is not any lack of "taste"; it is rather an inhibiting excess of it.

THE STORY OF
EUGENE GANT

It is true enough in a sense to maintain that all his life Wolfe wrote only one novel. The hero, whether titanic and called Eugene, or simian and called George, is still Wolfe, and his adventures are Wolfe's adventures either in fact or in desire. It will be demonstrated later how the change of name came about and how, by running the four novels together, omitting the first sixteen chapters of *The Web and the Rock* and the various "short stories"that are incorporated in the text, it would be possible to present them as one entire work.

There are, however, two objections to this. The first is that though George is not in himself different from Eugene, the change brings about a certain shifting of emphasis. The books concerning Eugene are in the main more objective than those concerning George—though Wolfe, in fact, intended quite the opposite result. Eugene is seldom quite so important as the people around him and he remains their interpreter; but the people around George are set there to illumine George with their radiance, not he to illumine them. The second objection is that the two first books exhibit a certain native optimism springing clear and straight from Wolfe's early youth. He never drifted into total pessimism; but in the later books his hope arises rather from a wish to hope and a refusal to despair than from any fundamental buoyancy of spirit.

In accordance with these objections, the following analysis of the structure and action of the books is made in two groupings: the story of Eugene Gant, and the story of George Webber.

Look Homeward Angel, in common with the other novels, takes its keynote from a brief prose-poem.

"Naked and alone we came into exile. In her dark womb we did not know our mother's face; and from the prison of her flesh have we come into the unspeakable and incommunicable prison of the earth."

Oliver Gant, a big, vulnerable man of inchoate and unstable longings, a seeker after poetry and the answer to inexpressible questions, desires to carve the face of an angel. To that end he becomes apprenticed to a stonemason and in time becomes a craftsman, but his desire is never realised.

"He never found it. He never learned to carve an angel's head. The dove, the lamb, the smooth joined marble hands of death and letters fair and fine—but not the angel."

His son Eugene is also to search for this art; to carve in words the angel whose lips speak the answer to all questions and fold upon the satisfaction of all longings.

Gant comes to Altamont, the small mountain town of Old Catawba, where he marries his second wife, Eliza Pentland, a trim, sharp-eyed, sharp-tongued woman from a fantastical Scotch-English family.

Here Wolfe develops the two linked themes: Gant's rhetorical, Lyceum drunkenness, and Eliza's steady childbearing. Eugene is her seventh, and by six years her youngest, child.

The story now passes into Eugene's consciousness, telling of his childhood, his "queerness", his early literary influences, the small miracle of how he suddenly, one day, learned to write. His day-dreams, based upon cheap romantic fiction, are illustrated by some heavy-handed and funny *pastiche*. The humour in the earlier books is far broader than in the later. Eugene is sent out to peddle newspapers (this is the source of much misery and humiliation) and Eliza buys the boarding-house, *Dixieland*. Servants come and go. When they go, Eugene makes nightmare trips into the negro quarter to ferret out new ones. All his adventures are related on a prodigious, swollen scale; the child's world is peopled with monsters and giants, some beautiful, some hideous, some terrible, but all lurid with the inner burning of a mystery. At the end of Part I he is engaged upon the detested chore of "drumming-up business" for his mother's boarding establishment.

At twelve he discovers the humanity of his brother Ben. Ben has always seemed remote, the one to bark, to scowl, to shout about him to others over his head. Eugene now begins to realise that between him and this man there is a tie which is to be the most strait, yet the most sustaining, of his life. Ben is shown as if by sheet lightning in one of the most marvellous descriptive passages Wolfe ever wrote:

"My Brother Ben's face, thought Eugene, is like a piece of slightly yellow ivory; his high white head is knotted fiercely by his old man's scowl, his mouth is like a knife, his smile the flicker of light across a blade. His face is like a blade, and a knife, and a flicker of light: it is delicate and fierce and he scowls beautifully forever, and when he fastens his hard white fingers and his scowling eyes upon a thing he wants to fix, he sniffs with sharp and private concentration through his long pointed nose. Thus women, looking, feel a well of tenderness for his pointed, bumpy, always scowling face: his hair shines like that of a young boy—it is crinkled and crisp as a lettuce."

Through Ben, Eugene comes to know the young men of Altamont, the rakes, the loafers, the drunks, the fantastics, who are sketched here with such violence and rapidity that the pen seems to jag the paper. They are among the first influences of his adolescence.

The most important of all the influences, however, is Margaret Leonard, who, with her husband, keeps school in Altamont. She plays the first mother-role in Eugene's life, and is the prototype of all the women with whom he will fall deeply in love. "Margaret Leonard" was created in praise of Mrs. J. M. Roberts, who was his teacher in Asheville, and to whom he wrote letters remarkable in their enthusiastic affection and deep confidence. In a testimonial written to the Superintendent of Schools in Asheville he said:

". . . . With all the moderation and temperance and earnestness at my command I can do no less than consider Mrs. Roberts as one of the three great teachers who have ever taught me,—this with all honour to Harvard, who has not yet succeeded in adding a fourth name to my own Hall of Fame.

"I have spoken of Mrs. Roberts merely as a teacher. This is perhaps the only testimonial you want. But I cannot stop before I speak of another matter that has been of the highest importance to me. During the years Mrs. Roberts taught me she exercised an influence that is inestimable on almost every particular of my life and thought . . . I put the relation of a fine teacher to a student just below the relation of a mother to her son. . . ."*

* *Atlantic Monthly*, December, 1946.

[37]

To Mrs. Roberts herself he wrote, in a letter dated May 30th, 1937:

"You say that no one *outside* my family loves me more than Margaret Roberts. Let me rather say the exact truth: that no one *inside* my family loves me as much, and only one other person, I think, in all the world loves me as much. My book is full of ugliness and terrible pain—and I think moments of a great and soaring beauty. In it (will you forgive me?) I have told the story of one of the most beautiful people I have ever known as it touched my own life. I am calling that person Margaret Leonard.

". . . . I found you, when else I should have died, you mother of my spirit who fed me with light. Do you think that I have forgotten? Do you think I ever will? You are entombed in my flesh. You are in the pulses of my blood, the thought of you makes a great music in me—and before I come to death, I shall use the last thrust of my talent—whatever it is—to put your beauty into words."*

As a boy Eugene found Margaret Leonard; for the rest of his life, in all other women, he sought for her likeness.

Eugene is a brilliant boy. When he wins the essay prize the Leonards persuade Eliza to loosen her financial grip just far enough to enable her son to continue his schooling. In this section there is a cruel and touching study of the androgyne Jewish boy, Edward Michalove, so brutally persecuted by his schoolmates; the theme is later to be developed, with most beautiful elaboration, into the story of Frank Starwick in *Of Time and the River*.

Eugene is now growing conscious of sex. His earliest and most beastly experience, though it seems to leave no

* *Atlantic Monthly*, December, 1946.

psychic mark, comes to him when he surprises his degenerate brother Steve with one of Eliza's woman boarders. Steve, a character almost intolerably repellent and unlit by any spark of the charity so pervasive elsewhere in Wolfe's writing, symbolises the horror that Wolfe found in the closer family relationships. An emotional upheaval outside the family circle—a 'scene' with a woman, or with a close friend—could be brought to an end without leaving a shameful hangover; emotional crises within the family held always something dark, obscene, sickly and remotely incestuous. To these there could be no ending—only a change in the conversation, a quick powdering over the sore.

The first world war has broken out. Despite the æsthetic influence of Margaret Leonard, Eugene is rolled sweetly again into his fantasies, this time imagining himself returning to Altamont an armless hero, or lying exquisitely dead upon the field of battle. He is fifteen years of age when he has his first sexual experience with a pleasant and discreet little waitress at an hotel.

Part II ends with the revelation that Oliver Gant is dying of cancer.

Eugene, not quite sixteen, six feet three inches tall, goes to the State University. Fearing that, through some casual adventure, he has contracted a disease, he makes Ben take him to the doctor. The description of the boy's terrors as, under his brother's disbelieving scowl, he submits himself for examination and his enormous whooping relief when he finds his fears groundless, is masterly sour comedy.

In April of that year the nation declares war on Germany. Eugene, home on vacation, falls in love with Laura James, a girl some five years older than he, who is boarding at *Dixieland*. This affair is presented as an idyll, embroidered with some of Wolfe's most lush, but perhaps not most moving, poetic-prose. The background to the idyll—Eliza's disapproving pin-pricks, the nagging of the boy's sister Helen—is far more touching than the spectacle of the two leading figures, who, classically embraced in an Elysian landscape, have a Maxfield Parrish touch. Eugene is never able to make nor to record love in a manner that carries any deep conviction to the reader.

Laura goes home, explaining to the boy that she will be absent for a little while only, but shortly afterwards she writes him a farewell letter breaking the news of her approaching marriage. Relieved that Eugene is free of what they consider a ridiculous and precocious entanglement, Eliza and Helen torture him with their derision. Wretched, goaded, disillusioned, he consoles himself with another of Eliza's boarders, this time a shoddy woman who watches for young men as a cat for mice.

He returns to the university for his second year. While on vacation, he comes home to *Dixieland* drunk for the first time in his life, and precipitates the first major crisis of his adult experience. Eliza, Helen, Ben and the easy-going, stuttering brother Luke are terrified that Eugene will follow in the steps of the dipsomaniac father, and so, with one unified, nagging voice, they bring their disapproval to bear upon him. Eugene, driven beyond endurance, falls physically upon Ben and Luke, and there follows a crazy, shameful fight without Queensberry rules. He rounds upon his brothers, charging them with having shut him out of their lives.

" 'Have you ever told me anything of yourself? Have

you ever tried to be a friend or a companion to me?' "

For his mother he has the ancient cry of every child badgered by the awful demand for gratitude—Did I ask to be born? He tells them that at last he is free of them all, at last owing them nothing. Wolfe brings this scene to a close with one of the most sure and startling strokes he ever achieved.

" 'Now at last I am free from you all, although you may hold me for a few years more. If I am not free, I am at least locked up in my own prison, but I shall get me some beauty: I shall get me some order out of this jungle of my life: I shall find my way out of it yet, though it take me some twenty years more—alone.'

" 'Alone?' said Eliza, with the old suspicion. 'Where are you going?'

" 'Ah,' he said, 'you were not looking, were you? I've gone.' "

It is not wise to interpret altogether literally certain of Wolfe's conversations. This peroration of Eugene's actually spoken would be absurd; it could not survive upon a stage. What Wolfe does here, as not infrequently elsewhere, is to transcribe not the actual words spoken at a certain time, but the sum of an elaborate thought which he is unable to do more than indicate in the terms of literal speech. Very often in scenes of violent emotional stress it is the *thoughts* of Wolfe's characters which appear in the disguise of spoken words: this is his first, and most certainly his last, affinity with Compton Burnett.

Still obsessed by the memory of Laura James, Eugene goes in search of her. When money runs out he takes a job as a "checker" on a flying-field at Newport News. He gambles his wages, starves and falls ill, until one of the checkers befriends him and pulls him together. He decides that he is free now of Laura, so he abandons the search for her. He has, in fact, had a long anticipated nervous breakdown, and the release of stored tensions has done him good.

Returning to the University two weeks before his eighteenth birthday, when the war fever is at its height, he lives for the day when he can be accepted for military service. He is still romancing.

"He saw himself as Ace Gant, the falcon of the skies, with sixty-three Huns to his credit by his nineteenth year. He saw himself walking up the Champs Elysées, with a handsome powdering of grey hair above his temples, a left forearm of the finest cork, and the luscious young widow of a French marshal at his side. For the first time he saw the romantic charm of mutilation."

Then he is called home suddenly: his brother is dying of pneumonia. There are three deaths in literature comparable for power and pity and horror with the death of Ben: the death of Oliver Gant, in *Of Time and the River*, of the father in Roger Martin du Gard's *Les Thibault*, and of the grandmother in *A la Recherche du Temps Perdu*. The nervous strain of it, the appalling grief, and above all the pervasive *bad temper* are suggested with an extraordinary nakedness and force. The family wrangles, weeps and nags about the dying man. When the oxygen tank is brought Ben sees it as an object of incomprehensible torment.

"Eugene gripped Ben's hot wrists: his heart turned rotten. Ben rose wildly from his pillows, wrenching like a child to get his hand free, gasping horribly, his eyes wild with terror."

At last Helen asks the doctor if there is nothing more he can do.

"'I want to know. Is there anything left worth trying?' He made a weary gesture of his arms. 'My dear girl!' he said. 'He's drowning! Drowning!'"

The section ends in classic resignation, grey and solid, as static in pain and acceptance as the stone angel that hangs above the whole book. *Dixieland* is the sad house of King Admetus, and those that stand within it have the dignity of immortals.

After this, the cathartic, hysterical joke. Eugene: "'By God! That's one thing Ben's out of. He won't have to drink Mamma's coffee any more.'"

Then there is the wild, black, comic scene in the funeral parlour, where Horse Hines, with his stick of rouge, puts the finishing touches to Ben's cheeks. "'There are artists, boys, in every profession,' Horse Hines continued in a moment, with quiet pride."

The war ends; Eugene, though never "Ace Gant", never a romantic corpse upon some foreign field, is a great man in the university, though perhaps not altogether a popular one. He is "queer", he "doesn't bath" . . . The world is beginning to weave his legend from the silk he so assiduously spins for it.

He has discovered upon the back of his neck the "small tetter of itch", the Pentland "brand". It is the symbol of his pride, his shame, his aloofness. He grows his hair long in order to hide it, or perhaps, like the lawyer-duke in Chesterton's story, to draw attention to its existence. Because he is afraid of people in the mass, his vanity drives him to miching mallecho upon the individual.

"Remembering his savage fear and hatred of the crowd, with man alone he would play cruelly; like a

[43]

cat, snarling gently at him, prowling in on him softly, keeping cocked and silent the terrible tiger's paw of his spirit."

Wolfe has an unquenchable longing to be wicked, in the dark and grand manner. He did, in fact, strike spontaneous sympathy and affection from everyone he met, and found it hard to keep an enemy. The boy is forgiven where the man is held responsible, and it was the boyish strain in Wolfe which in Eugene is expressed both in collegiate exhibitionism and in the cautious, hinted speculations as to whether he may or may not be a genius.

When he graduates from the State University he decides that he must go to Harvard.

Helen is married now, childless, bitterly bored with her husband. Gant is dying. Steve pays another of his foul and terrifying visitations.

In the final chapter realism is abandoned entirely. The abandonment does not come as a shock, and for this reason: throughout the book it has been hinted. It has been hinted in the conversations that were spoken thoughts, the incidents reddened by a light that never was on land or sea, the symbols of angel and of scar. Walking by moonlight in the square at Altamont, Eugene encounters the ghost of Ben, which stands, smoking a cigarette, on the portico beside the stone angel. Ben speaks. The angel moves.

"With a strong rustle of marble and a cold sigh of weariness, the angel nearest Eugene moved her stone foot and lifted her arm to a higher balance. The slender lily stipe shook stiffly in her elegant cold fingers."

Ben, in bitter, sarcastic love, tells Eugene that when he goes away, when he leaves for the city, he will never come back. " 'Do you know why you are going or are you just taking a ride on the train?' " He tells him there is no more to be found in life than the life he has known till now; there is no world save in himself. But Eugene, with the Prometheus-optimism of youth, will not believe even the authoritative word of a ghost, who must know all things. He looks out in leaping hope towards the future.

From this point onwards, the novel is called *Of Time and the River*.

Before the usual prose-poem, Wolfe has quoted as epigraph the three verses of *Kennst du das Land, wo die Zitronen blühn*. It is the promise of the "Dark Helen in my heart forever burning", the land of Germany to which Eugene will at last come, but in the body of George Webber, and in George Webber's cycle of experience.

The whole of the first part of this second volume is taken up by the train journey from Catawba to Boston. As originally conceived it was the length of a whole novel; even now, there is matter for a novel within it. It begins with the last collective portrait of the Gants and Pentlands, aligned in affection, envy and grudging pride against the boy who is about to escape them; if they had half a chance they would stamp quickly upon the wings which have sprung at last to his heels, and pin him to Altamont earth forever. The whole long episode is conceived in a kind of raging ecstasy. The train that bears Eugene out of the south is Leviathan, swimming and roaring majestically out of Carolina, out of Virginia, out of Maryland into the enchanted East.

Eugene has travelling companions, two business men and a politician of his acquaintance, who discuss the Gant family with that surprising and brutal knowledge often possessed by outsiders. As they speak of Ben, Eugene recalls how his brother scowlingly gave him a watch "to keep time with", a symbol to set beside the angel and the scar. He falls in with the tormented, uproarious young man Robert Weaver, and is goaded by Weaver's sadic tongue into a drinking bout. There is another brief outbreak of Joyce *pastiche* at this point, well enough done, but an excrescence upon the flesh of the story.

Now there is a flight backwards a few hours into time. In the early morning of Eugene's departure, Oliver Gant was dying in the sunlight of a hospital porch. He was dreaming of Time and of the world of youth, of his meeting with the Pentland tribe, and of his association with his wife's Uncle Bacchus, the malodorous, idiot saint, "the fated and chosen of God, the supernatural appearer on roads at nightfall, the harbinger of death, the prophet, chanting even then his promises of Armageddon and the Coming of the Lord." Gant's sons, Eugene and Luke, came to see him. It was an embarrassing hour for them, and it made Luke's stutter worse. And Eugene had a train to catch.

So Eugene, coming at last to the city and to the end of his journey, knows that his father's journey is also at an end. In all Wolfe's novels life proceeds from one conclusion to another; from the death of one period in human experience to the birth, the withering-away, and the death of the next.

In Boston the young man prowls the library stacks at night,

> "Pulling books out of a thousand shelves and reading them like a madman . . . He read insanely, by the hundreds, the thousands, the ten thousands . . . a

ravening appetite to him demanded that he read everything that had ever been written about human experience. He read no more from pleasure—the thought that other books were waiting for him tore at his heart for ever. He pictured himself tearing the entrails from a book as from a fowl."

It appears to him that he is upon the threshold of some stupendous and blazing adventure, that he holds the key to the whole earth and the whole of human possibility. "It seemed to him that he saw everything at once."

Then he receives a curt and cryptic note from Francis Starwick, the assistant of Professor Hatcher, whose play-writing class Eugene attends, asking him to dinner. Starwick, a pleasant-looking, brusque, precious young man who receives all confidences and returns none, gives the young Eugene a baffling and magical evening which, however, ends in a curious coldness and disappointment. It is months before he speaks with Starwick again.

At this point Wolfe begins to slot through his narrative the story of Bascom Pentland, Eugene's uncle, who lives in Boston. This is a cut version of *The Story of Bascom Hawke*, which was published as a short novel in 1932. It is a massive and violent comic episode, but it is not essential to the mainstream of Eugene's development and could easily be deleted in any telescoping of the four novels into a whole.

There follows a sardonic and delightful account of Professor Hatcher's class, which is attended by young people in a most concentrated state of adolescent superiority. All the portraits are small, glittering, and flushed with the light that Wolfe was always able to shed upon his minor characters, making them, if not important, unforgettable—to be remembered by their faces, which are not described, rather than by their words, which are meticulously recorded. The story returns to Bascom Pentland, and then tracks Eugene through a variety of intellectual, social and spiritual experiences recreated with feverish gusto. There is more sustained comedy in *Of Time and the River* than in any other of the volumes.

Eugene visits a girl of whom Bascom has spoken, a pleasant, dowdy, honest creature who lives with an honest, dowdy, stupid family. Out of an innate sadic tendency to play the devil with people of slow wits, Eugene presents himself to these innocents as a person of tremendous drama, a character to be heralded with the rattle of iron sheeting and the blaze of magnesium flares. It is all quite splendid until they find him out, and administer a rebuke all the more salutary because it arises from so great a simplicity. This whole episode is an apology, made with the generosity that arises only from the conviction of having been entirely in the wrong, unassisted to the fault and absolutely responsible for it.

The story now returns to Altamont for an intensive study of Eugene's sister Helen, and for the second of Wolfe's great death-scenes. Gant dies like a giant, in circumstances of gigantic pity and terror. This sequence is more sternly conceived than the earlier one which related to the death of Ben, and is much more protracted. It is also the more bearable of the two, for it is softened by the reconciliation of Gant and his wife, a woman not fitted for tragedy, but compelled perpetually to sup with it. Eliza is old and plain and shabby now, and her store of words small and thin; yet some provident and temporary greatness enables her to accept Gant's apology in the only way he would have found endurable—which is to reject it only in part. In this scene she is beautiful and noble, even her foolish, impenetrable optimism contributing to the comfort she alone is able to give the calmly-dying man.

In the meantime Starwick has become Eugene's closest friend. It is a friendship built rather upon some mysterious sympathy than upon any real understanding. At the conclusion of Book II Eugene makes his first protest against the secrecy which is deeply-sunken in Starwick's nature. Starwick is sufficiently moved to tell him some half-truths, to hint at the miseries of his youth, to hint at the agony of the "naked man" beneath the arrogant and nervous æsthete. It costs him a hideous effort to say even so much, and Eugene knows it. For the moment he is satisfied.

Eugene believes that he will become a great writer. At home he is racked by the deadly tensions of the domestic atmosphere and by his family's grinning disbelief in his future. While visiting his other married sister in South Carolina he meets Robert Weaver again, and is dragged by him into a drunken episode that lands both young men in jail. This incident, beginning as comedy, ends in "something dark, grey and terrible". Eugene loses control of his *instincts:* he has always thought he knew what they were, and he now discovers that he was deceived. Locked in a cell with a negro, a submerged and unsuspected colour-feeling roars up in a flood of shame and degradation. He is sick with horror at the stranger who stands within himself.

Eliza does not nag him about this lapse as about his earlier drunken freak; half-reconciled with her, even as his father had been, he leaves for New York to become English instructor at the university. He is twenty-three years old.

"After these months of frenzy, drunkenness and arrest, he was at the last gasp of his resources, and the eighteen hundred dollars a year . . . seemed to him a wage of princely munificence—a stroke of incredible good fortune."

Here, in fear and contempt, his own dread of the "crowd" making him shake and tremble as if with ague, he tries to drum a love of literature into thick and ugly and derisive heads, Jewish heads for the most part—or so his deep-lying anti-Semitism assures him—and one of them the head of Abe Jones. Eugene hates Abe, not for his stupidity, but for his awful, bowelless, profitless talent. Abe is the one who knows, who criticises, who complains. He complains to Eugene once too often, at which the goaded instructor threatens him with expulsion from the class. Abe instantly falls into distress, takes off his glasses and agitatedly wipes away the dimming of tears.

"His grey ugly face as he stood there polishing his glasses had that curiously naked, inept, faded and tired wistful look that is common to people with weak eyes when they remove their spectacles; it was a good and ugly face, and suddenly Eugene began to like Abe very much."

It is typical of Wolfe that this study should begin in hatred and be concluded in love. It is remarkable observation of a familiar but seldom analysed type, the striving and despised intellectual taking out his poor satisfactions in writing sadistic-emotional letters to a friend, and receiving the abusive replies with crows of delight. Abe Jones, given a family, money and the right friends, would lie at no great a distance from Bloch, in *A la Recherche du Temps Perdu*,—except that Abe would never have possessed quite enough persistence to change his whole physical appearance and appear in the salons as Jacques du Rozier. Abe is forever Abe, the man of great talent rendered sterile by a single spoiling element, the man who will strive all his life and get nowhere at all.

In the city Eugene is visited by Robert Weaver and involved again in this damned soul's dissipations, though this time as a keeper rather than as a boon companion. He renews a Cambridge acquaintance with Joel Pierce, the son of a millionaire family, and at his invitation goes to stay at the mansion on the Hudson river. It is Eugene's first contact with the Rich. For various reasons, of a fairly complex nature, he brings his friendship with Joel to an abrupt end and returns from "that world of moonlight, magic and painted smoke" to the world of struggle and poverty and hard reality.

Although Starwick, the most radiant, subtle and pitiful of Wolfe's characters, dominates the whole of Part V, which, in accord with the Joycean-Homeric subtitling used throughout the book is called *Jason's Voyage*, it is not necessary to make more than a brief summary of his story.

Eugene goes to Europe: first to England, which he sees as fog-bound, exclusive, dowdy and rotten with pride, whose traditions he despises while he envies and admires, and then to Paris. Lonely, working madly, reading madly, making—it is interesting to note—no contact with the American literary colony, he encounters Starwick one day, standing exquisite upon the steps of the Louvre. Starwick is travelling with two Boston women. Elinor, the elder, is married, and has run away from her husband to accompany throughout Europe the young man who is so fascinating and unpredictable a companion. She is a curious creature, on the surface splendid and jolly, full of wit, a smoother of paths and a speaker of the right word at the right time, but under the surface of her devotion to Starwick Eugene senses something murky, perverse and sad.

Ann is handsome, heavy-faced and silent, beautiful only when she laughs, but then beautiful beyond all other women. Her attitude towards Starwick is sardonic and exasperated; it is much the same towards Eugene. Starwick sponges for money on both women, but upon Ann in particular. Eugene is drawn into this odd, shuttered circle and within it leads the racketing nightmare life, shot through with lightnings, blotted out by crapulas, of Gershwin's *American in Paris*. Underneath the gaiety, the sickness, the tedium, the hysteric flare-up of pleasure, evil thickens. Eugene falls in love with Ann, to find that she has given her own love, calmly, knowledgeably, hopelessly, to Starwick. The shock and disappointment force Eugene to admit consciously a fact he has always known, but which he has driven down below the water-line: the nature of Starwick's misery. In a beastly frenzy of jealousy he throws his knowledge in Starwick's face and knocks him down. It is the end of the friendship; but Wolfe adds one of his characteristic codas. For the last time the young men talk things out, and here, as in the episode of Eugene's rejection of his family, the dialogue is heightened out of realism. These are things felt, not things said.

Starwick makes his agonised plea for understanding.

"'. . . . Oh, to feel so, suffer so, and live so!—however mistaken you may be! . . . To have come lusty, young, and living into this world . . . not to have come, like me, still-born from your mother's

womb—never to know the dead heart and the passion-
less passion—the cold brain and the cold hopelessness
of hope—to be wild, mad, furious, and tormented—
but to have belief, to live in anguish, but to live—
and not to die.'

". . . He turned and opened the door. 'I would
give all I have and all you think I have, for just one
hour of it. You call me fortunate and happy. *You* are
the most fortunate and happy man I ever knew.
Good-bye, Eugene.'

" 'Good-bye, Frank. Good-bye, my enemy.'

" 'And good-bye, my friend,' said Starwick. He
went out, and the door closed behind him."

Eugene wanders over France working, struggling,
going broke, profiting briefly by the schemings of a
crazy-shrewd Frenchwoman who loves all things
American and has persuaded herself that Eugene is a
great man who writes for the *New York Times*. The book
is rushing out of darkness now like a train out of a
tunnel. Eugene's youth, his buoyancy, his optimism
are observing once more the red nose of the tragedian,
the cat that strolls across the stage as Medea appears in
the dragon car upon the roof. The humour inclines
more steeply towards the dark, the grotesque, than in
the days of Professor Hatcher's class; but it is still a
force for survival and endeavour.

The memory of America now returns in a flood, filling
Eugene's thoughts with love and desire. He feels the
passing of Time, is conscious always of the ticking of
the watch Ben gave him.

" 'To keep time with!' To Eugene Gant, Presented
to Him on the Occasion of his Twelfth Birthday, by
His Brother B. H. Gant, October 3, 1912 . . . 'To

keep time with!' . . . Up on the mountain, down in the valley, deep, deep in the hill, Ben, cold, cold, cold.''

This is the last and most brief of the threnodies with which the novel is adorned and black-bordered.

One day Eugene catches sight of Starwick, Elinor and Ann in a Marseilles café, and he flies from them like a man pursued by furies. He is haunted by their nearness to himself, for so long as all four are penned together in the same world, these lost friends will yet be too near. For him their story is ended: and will live in him as long as he lives.

He is going home, home to America. On the tender that takes the passengers out to the great ship, lying blazing with light on the grey ocean, a woman looks eagerly out to the moment of meeting.

'' 'Oh, look!' the woman cried again. 'Oh, see! Was ever anything more beautiful?' The ship's great beetling cliff swept sheer above her. She turned the small, flushed flower of her face and saw the slant and reach and swell of the great prow, and music filled her.''

She is passionate with the violence of her thoughts, groping for words to contain them. Eugene looks at her and loves her. In that first second he might have seen her as she was in reality—"the pleasant image of the woman that perhaps she was, and that life saw. He never knew. He only knew that from that moment his spirit was impaled upon the knife of love.''

Her name is Esther.

She is for Eugene the Dark Helen of his search, the Dark Helen which is now a woman, but is one day to become a Land; and for many years she is to be loved by Eugene Gant, who is now to become George Josiah Webber.

THE STORY OF
GEORGE WEBBER

ALL that is fundamental in Wolfe is in Eugene Gant.
As Starwick says—"The whole thing's there—it really
is!" It is remarkable how little the Wolfe hero develops
with time. At a point there comes a stop, after which
experience has no power to affect the character beyond a
certain narrow limit. By his eighteenth year the hero is
complete. He has paused upon the far border of
boyhood, and he never really moves on. Because of this
and because, with the exception of the first ten chapters
of *The Web and the Rock*, George's story runs roughly
parallel with Eugene's, it would be superfluous to
analyse the action of the second group of novels in very
great detail.

For George, Wolfe creates a new family background.
George Josiah Webber, of Libya Hill, Old Catawba, is
the son of a brick-mason and general builder. John
Webber's marriage is a wretched one. Eight years after
the birth of George, an only child, he leaves his wife for
a young woman who has been his mistress, in some
dubious secrecy, for a year or more. Amelia Webber
divorces her husband, and young George, stigmatised
by this disgrace, is sent to live with his uncle, Mark
Joyner, and Mark's pious Baptist wife Mag. It is a
dismal household for a boy, and Aunt Maw, his "dark
old aunt of doom", a "rusty crone of fate", who has the
spirit if not the rhetorical powers of Queen Margaret in
Richard III, is chief darkener of his days.

In some submerged and knowing part of his mind, while the upper reaches of thought appreciate the sweetness of lying on grass upon a fair day, George Webber meditates upon the North and the South.

"Old Catawba is much better than South Carolina. It is more North, and 'North' is a much more wonderful word than 'South', as anyone with any ear for words will know."

In South Carolina they drawl beautifully, are graceful and warm, but are afraid.

"Their eyes are desperately afraid, filled with a kind of tortured and envenomed terror of the old, stricken, wounded 'southness' of cruelty and lust."

The men stand about the drug stores making their fraternal, corny jokes, but now and then they go and lynch a negro, killing him with a kind of squirming, lunatic brutality. In Old Catawba

" . . . the hillmen kill . . . in drunkenness or in the red smear of the murder lust. But they do not saw off niggers' noses. There is not the look of fear and cruelty in their eyes that the people in South Carolina have."

Wolfe managed to come to terms with his "Southness." He was never forced to cry, as Faulkner cried through the mouth of Quentin Compson—"I don't. I don't! I don't hate it. I don't hate it!"—because his love for it was not sufficiently strong to veer to the opposing pole of disgust. The fact that he was of North rather than of South Carolina seemed to him just right. He was just "north" enough to be saved from the diseases of pride and fear and defeat that raddle the spirit of Faulkner. The borderline had saved him, and he felt himself secure behind it as behind the Great Wall of China.

George Webber, midway to thirteen, has a simian look; the boys call him Monk.

"Not large or heavy for his age, but strong and heavy in the shoulders, arms absurdly long, big hands, legs thin, bowed out a little, long, flat feet; small face and features quick with life, the eyes deep-set, their look both quick and still; low brow, wide. stick-out ears; a shock of close-cropped hair, a large head that hangs forward and projects almost too heavily for the short thin neck—not much to look at—someone's ugly duckling, just a boy."

So Wolfe disguised his fine body and face that might have been painted upon the ceiling of the Sistine chapel: and did it with a signal success as the comedian who in *Dick Whittington* disguises himself as the cat.

Other boys are introduced—the cruel and bullying boys Sid, Carl and Harry, and George's lifelong friend Nebraska Crane, who is all that is good and honest and brave. Aunt Maw is castigated in a blistering section devoted to her. Various incidents that stand out upon the blur of George's youth like lights upon a river at night are elaborated one by one without interrelation, and are followed by two complete short stories: *The Butcher* and *Child by Tiger*. The first is the tale of horrible parents and a horrible son, who are seen by George through the magnifying glass of uncomprehending terror. The second, which is as violent and as pitiful, tells of a negro who ran amok with a gun (a quiet man once, a good and consoling man), was pursued, captured, and slain.

One September day in 1916 George goes to the State University. His father has left him an inheritance just large enough to take him through college. Here he meets new friends, Jim Randolph, a great baseball player, and Randy Shepperton. Jim goes to the war, returns a hero; but his spine is injured, and though his name and fame are as lustrous as before, somehow he is regarded with pity and regret.

"He had suffered the sad fate of men who live to see themselves become a legend. And now the legend lived. The man was just a ghost to them."

George falls under the influence of a merry, hearty, Bible-thumper called Gerald Alsop, who loves Dickens for all the wrong reasons and hounds George out of the college literary set when the latter, in trembling defiance, champions Dostoievski. Gerald Alsop is a more intelligent, a more dangerous 'Old Jud Roberts',* and Wolfe's charity is extended to him with reserve.

George comes to New York and lives there in an apartment house with five friends, including the desperate and ruined Jim Randolph. Alsop comes to the city too, and he and George are temporarily reconciled; but in the end Alsop turns upon him with that hatred disguised beneath a joke which Wolfe attacks at all times as the vilest form of human vengeance. George has begun to write.

"The subject he chose for his first effort was a boy's vision of life over a ten month period between his twelfth and thirteenth year, and the title was *The End of the Golden Weather*."

It is his first, naïve pride in being an "artist" that provokes Alsop to the intolerable outrage.

Upon this raw and remarkable scene another follows: it is one of Wolfe's highest and most sad pieces of irony. The four youths with whom Jim Randolph lives are growing tired of the shoddy round of racketing,

* Sinclair Lewis: *Elmer Gantry*.

drinking and woman-chasing. They are boys, shallow, silly, but full of hope and promise: Randolph is a man for whom everything worth-while has ended, and he sees their defection from the frantic pleasures of his ruined life as the symbol of final defeat. One night he announces that he has been appointed by a news agency to some obscure post in South America.

"He was bitterly, resentfully triumphant. He was going, he said, to 'get out of this damn town and tell them all to go to hell'. In another month or two he'd be in South America, where a man could do as he blank, blank pleased, without being watched and hindered all the time. To hell with all of them anyway! He'd lived long enough to find out one thing for himself— that most of the people who call themselves your friends are nothing but a bunch of crooked, double-crossing blank, blank, blanks, who stabbed you in the back the moment your back was turned. Well, to hell with 'em and the whole country! They could take it and——

"Bitterly he drank, and drank again."

Jim, in an ugly mood, demands that the usual girls shall be sought out and brought in; "but even they, the whole shabby carnival of them, had turned on Jim at last." There are no girls. There is nothing to do but drink. Dexter Briggs, "a little, amiably good-natured newspaper drunk," sits at Jim's typewriter composing elegies. In the middle of a furious quarrel, while Jim accuses the boys of betraying and double-crossing him, Dexter, weeping gently, taps out this reproachful verse and reads it to them:

"Boys, boys,
　　Be Southern gentlemen,

[59]

Do not say such things to one another,
  For, boys, boys,
You are Southern gentlemen,
  Southern gentlemen all."

Jim, madly drunk and raging, abusing his friends, flings his empty gin glass at the wall, where it smashes into fragments.

"Southern gentlemen, all," Dexter recites sadly and collapses over the keys, the defeated upholder of the ancient traditions of other people. Jim slams out, his last soiled glory departing. When the light of it, however lurid, however minatory a light, has faded, the friendship of the young men disintegrates. Jim has held the admiration of crowds, and lost it. At the end he held the admiration of four young men, and he has lost that also; and now they have nothing more to say to one another. The misery of this farewell party, heightened by the flashes of sour and hectic comedy, is conveyed with that extraordinary economy of word and phrase which the verbose and florid Wolfe could, when he chose, command. It is one of the great "small scenes" of the book.

Living alone now in careful squalor, George solaces himself with a new and elaborate fantasy, in which he is a poor young author who, through the act of returning a lost handbag, is taken up by a beautiful rich woman who falls madly in love with him. It is the highly-coloured anticipation of the Esther-reality; it is very young and very touching. He even thinks of the food she will cook for him, and the image of tender three-inch strips of steak, mealy fried potatoes and young boiled onions, deep-dish apple pie, coffee strong and fragrant with heavy cream, brings water to his mouth and his eyes. He will pay fifteen dollars a week for his board, he decides, so that he may keep his self-respect, and will spend his days in the most marvellous library in the world. He will be loved and secure. All day he will work furiously. At night he will "dine with rich hunger and thirst, and, through the hours of darkness, lie in the restorative arms of his beautiful mistress".

The twopence-coloured style in which this fantasy is related is perhaps a half-hearted reaction to the Gerty McDowell episode in *Ulysses;* but it is not imitative and there is no sneer in it. It is a dream dressed in the poetry of grand absurdities, warmed by its very trustfulness. On the printed page, both a dream and a reality may be equally real to a reader; only on a page may the desire and the fulfilment meet, not a pin to choose between them. It is in this fashion that the young writer solaces himself—by writing down the process of his dream which, on the leaf of the book, shines in no greater brightness and in no different colour from the record of his actual experience. Both are made permanent in black and white. The democracy of print makes equal to the reader's eye the wish and the fact.

George Webber goes upon his Jason's voyage, ravening back and forth across Europe in fury and hunger, until the longing for return drives him homeward again. In 1926, on the Italian ship *Vesuvia*, he meets Esther Jack. In the third class he has made an acquaintance, a sporting goods salesman called Plemmons who is the life and soul of the dining saloon, a man so self-assured that he goes boldly up to the first class for a swim. "Up there," he tells George, he has met two beautiful ladies. He adds that he is going "up" after dinner and will take George also.

[61]

"One of these women is a fine and talented person
. . . who takes a great interest in the theatre and knows
all kinds of people in New York that you might like
to know."

The meeting takes place. One of the women is called
Lily, a person of "sensational and even formidable
appearance". She greets George coldly. Then Esther
comes in, little and jolly-faced and rosy. For perhaps a
couple of hours George is able to see her as she really is.
(He does not fall in love quite so spontaneously as
Eugene.) After that he is so much in love with her that
for him she is simply beauty incarnate, before whose
image all other women must seem coarse and stale.

One of the many complex reasons that bring George
back to New York is the need to earn money. Upon his
return he becomes English instructor at the School of
Utility Cultures. After a while his longing to see Esther
once more prompts him to write her a long, pompous,
self-deceiving letter, the theme of which is that he would
not object to renewing the acquaintance so long as she
realises that he has no intention of "truckling" to the
rich. Perceiving the desperate longing beneath this
farrago, Esther invites him to meet her at the smart little
East Side theatre in which she is a power. During the
performance she takes him backstage, where he meets
the theatrical people who make up the most important
part of her world.

There are some persons who find it an experience
fascinating but repellent to be taken "behind the scenes",
and Wolfe appears to have been one of them. The
repulsion arises partly from a feeling of being "shut
out", an alien in a very secret world, partly from the
daubed ugliness of stage make-up at close quarters, and

partly from an idea that people in disguise can make us ridiculous by their very security beneath the wigs and the paint. They have us at a disadvantage. They see us naked, as we are; we can only guess at the truth of them. We are in much the same position as the man beneath the bright light who is interrogated by the man in darkness. Wolfe wanted to see all people plain; he offered himself plainly to them and demanded confidence for confidence. It was for his disguise that Eugene finally came to hate Frank Starwick. It is because he fears the world working secretly in masquerade that George Webber turns with such instinctive hostility upon Esther's friends.

After the performance she teases him about his letter, so creating an intimacy between them: but little more is said. On his birthday they meet again. They dine and drink, and by nightfall George is violently, rhetorically drunk. He turns against the world, even against Esther. He accuses her of deserting him, betraying him. Finally he gets out of the car, slams the door upon her, and reels back exhausted, hopeless and sick to his hotel.

In the morning she telephones him, mild, friendly, without rebuke. They meet again and all is resolved.

"Then they came together and he put his arms around her and she put her arms around his neck and they kissed each other on the mouth."

Mrs. Jack has a wealthy husband and a grown-up daughter, with neither of whom is her life much involved. A brilliant stage-designer, she finds an all-absorbing existence beyond the walls of her home. She takes a flat in an old house as a work-place for herself and as a refuge for herself and George. He is happy. Everywhere she goes she carries with her a sense "of health, of life, of work, of human understanding". He almost adjusts himself to her rich Jewish friends, her theatrical friends, her successful intellectual friends; but he feels that in the background of her life there is something old and evil and corrupt, and slowly this poison begins to work in him. Yet for a long while their raptures continue; the joy over work, over loving, over food; the wild and cannibalistic endearments. George has begun the writing of his book and has made his entry into what, in a resentful passage, he calls the "mysteries of *la vie littéraire*." He is at odds with it: with the publishers who, he believes, prey upon the writers (there is a long section of satire, too vindictive to be really amusing, upon the publishing house of "Rawng and Wright",) with the authors who have succeeded despite their inferiority to himself, and with all the crowd of hangers-on who glitter about the world of letters.

He has begun now to torment Esther, his violence growing into ugliness. He taunts her with her race, her wealth, even with her talent. Once, after he has thrown her out of the flat, she creeps back again to bribe him into reconciliation with the promise of the fine meal she will cook for him; but it is only a temporary readjustment. The way to his heart is not entirely through his stomach.

George thinks of nothing but his vast manuscript and his rejection slips. Esther is doing all she can for him, but her efforts go for nothing. George's mind is darkening, and is eaten by many hatreds. After another long and hideous quarrel he thrusts her out of the flat and fancies himself rid of her forever, but again remorse overtakes him.

"He struck his fist into his face, a wild and wordless cry was torn from his throat, and he rushed from his room and from the house, out in the street to find her."

The writing of this section is blustering and hysterical, at best like the worst of Emily Brontë, and at worst (which is more frequent) like third-rate Victorian melodrama. Wolfe's visual sense seems to desert him here. The picture of George smashing himself in the face, giving a "wordless cry" and plunging for the street does not merely approach the ludicrous; it overruns it. The whole chronicle of these quarrels and reconciliations is prolonged, repetitive and tedious, narrowing down the interest to two persons who are already over-familiar and have little more to reveal concerning themselves.

In the quarrel that precedes the long parting, George tells Esther he is through with her forever.

". . . Their life was finished, he wanted to forget her utterly, to tear and strip her very memory from his blood, his brain, his heart, and go away somewhere, away from this accursed city, where he could gather up the shattered fragments of his life and build it back anew to a single integrity of purpose and design. He'd go to Europe—that's what he'd do!—put a wide ocean there between them, and let its raging waters wash away the last remaining vestige of all their life together, and it would then be just as though the two of them had never met and loved and lived and cursed and fought!"

The real trouble, unexpressed in these last collegiate rantings of a "single integrity of purpose and design", is two-fold. In the first place, George is tired of Esther's mothering. It has enabled him to complete his novel in comfort, and his debt to it is limitless: but it has served its purpose and he wants to cut the apron strings. (In a sense this is a parable of the literary break with Maxwell Perkins* and is interesting as a sidelight upon Wolfe's mental resistance where any form of guidance or supervision was concerned.) In the second place, George is driven by his pride—which is really a ramping inferiority-complex—to turn away from successful people until such time as he can feel that he is meeting them upon equal terms.

At the end of the academic year, George leaves for Europe. As he boards the boat at midnight he finds a letter from Esther awaiting him. It is angry, pathetic, resigned. It is full of attempts to do again the things for which he is leaving her—to mother him, advise him, patronise him. He tears the letter up and throws the fragments into the sea.

Though he flies from Esther, he cannot forget her. He strides the world like an exacerbated Colossus from one Poste Restante to the next, hoping for the word from her which never arrives. When he has rampaged through England and France he comes at last to Germany, and to the October Fair at Munich which was to have given Wolfe's second novel its name.

Germany is the magical land of great moons and shadows. Wolfe writes about it in a manner that ranges from his most intoxicating lyricism to his most guzzling fervour. George Webber is hypnotised now by the myth of Blood and Soil, dear to his heart, but to be overthrown at last by his intellect. Germany is the heaven of the voracious; it gorges the body and the mind. "That swarming multitude of Gothic print, that staggering superflux of German culture, maddened him with an intolerable and impossible hunger for possession." He

* See Appendix A.

would, if he could, eat books as he eats chicken and sausage and roast pig, the cherry and peach tarts, the "chocolates and bonbons, the candies and the crystal fruits, the glacéed plums and cherries and the cubes of pineapple, the brandied chocolates and the fragrant gums".

Yet even now he feels—he would not be George if he did not—something oppressive and evil beneath the roaring, extravagant and beaming life about him.

"He was horribly involved, caught up, entangled, in the Laocoön coils of his own madness. He wanted to satiate himself upon that which was itself unable to be fed, he wanted to assuage himself upon the unassuageable, appease himself upon the unappeasable, come to the end of all Unendlichkeit, unweave the swarming web, unthread to its last filament the texture of a pattern which could have no end. He wanted to possess in its entirety, fathom in its profundity, utter in its finality, that which was in itself unpossessable, unfathomable, and unutterable—the old Germanic and swarm-haunted mind of man."

The October Fair is described in Wolfe's most dominating manner: it is all richness and fear, crowded with huge jolly faces that imperceptbly come to wear the snouts of swine.

"Again there had been the roaring tumult of the people rising from their tables, linking arms together with their mugs upraised, the rhythmic swinging, the rocking back and forth to the blaring of 'Ein Prosit!' Again the ritualistic spell of all those human rings in swaying, roaring, one-voiced chant there in that vast and murky hall; again the image of the savage faces in the old dark forest of barbaric time; again the sudden fear of them that froze his heart. What happened then he did not know. In that quick instant of his drunken fear, had he swung out and smashed his great stone mug into the swinelike face, the red pig's eyes, of the hulking fellow next to him? He did not know, but there had been a fight—a murderous swinging of great mugs, a flash of knives, the sudden blinding fury of red, beer-drunk rage.''

He wakes in a Munich hospital, at last at peace with himself. The urgency of fear, so strong with him during his drunkenness at the Fair, has fled. "His fears were phantoms of his dark imagining, and he knew this now."

He is to discover this fear again, on his next visit to Germany two years after the coming of Hitler to power, is to comprehend that the evil thing brushed by the antennæ of his senses was the dark force out of which Fascism already had begun to swarm into the soul of a people. For the moment, however, and for the first time in many years, he is at rest and without terror.

In the city, which is the Rock upon which George Webber has spun the web of his experience, Esther sits on a park bench waiting for his return. He has written to her; she knows that "his lost body" now lies "battered and broken in a foreign land". She has been drinking all day and has eaten nothing. A policeman speaks to her. "It's time you were in bed, young lady. Where do you live?"

Esther answers (improbably, somewhat in the style of Sean O'Casey): "I have no home, for home is where the heart is, and the heart has been taken out of me, the heart has gone out of me entirely, and I am left alone here to die in the dark."

He asks her if she is waiting for anyone, and if so, what

this person looks like. "He has the face of a demented angel," she replies, "his head is wild and beautiful, and there is madness and darkness and evil in his brain." (It is curious to note here that Esther is giving a physical description of Eugene Gant, not of George Webber.) "He is more cruel than death, and more lovely than a flower. He is like a god, all made of light, and he lives alone in chains and darkness."

After a little more of this the policeman, not surprisingly, threatens to run her in. When she gives him her address, however, he is sufficiently impressed to escort her safely home by taxi.

The volume ends with a colloquy between George and his body on the subject of male beauty, and by George's coming-to-terms with the fact of his own ugliness. He and his simian flesh have discovered the earth together, and have learned one thing: "that they loved life and their fellow men and hated the death-in-life, and that it was better to live than to die."

From this point onwards the novel is called, *You Can't Go Home Again*.

George Webber is back in New York, back again with Esther being warmed by her, teased by her, mothered by her, adoringly gorged by her. He is very happy. One morning he is asked to call at the offices of James Rodney and Company, a distinguished publishing firm. He comes out from the interview dazed with joy, in his pocket a cheque for five hundred dollars advance against royalties. Foxhall Edwards, the editor, is his friend, and the finest man that ever was. *Home to Our Mountains* will be published soon.

While awaiting this event, George is compelled to return to Libya Hill for the funeral of Aunt Maw. Here he meets old acquaintances: Jarvis Riggs, the banker, amiable, weak Mayor Kennedy; "Parson" Flack, the local political boss; Nebraska Crane, now a baseball player in the big leagues and his name a household word, but as friendly, as generous as ever; and the blind and evil usurer Judge Rumford Bland. Judge Bland is "genuinely, unfathomably evil—and evil of this sort has a grandeur about it not unlike the grandeur of supreme goodness." In his noble and appalling person he symbolises the change and decay of Libya Hill; it is he who freezes George to the marrow by saying—"Do you think you can really go home again?" The young man is caught by a sickening consciousness of guilt. What has the judge heard? Has he heard about the book? Does he know the people of Libya Hill are in it? However, a stay with his friends Randy and Margaret Shepperton and the heady consciousness of being in a "Boom Town" —for Libya Hill is growing rapidly into riches and ugliness—stimulates him sufficiently to enable him to give an interview about his book to the local paper. The interview, when it appears, misrepresents him in a fashion that is later to prove disastrous.

"George Webber, son of the late John Webber and nephew of Mark Joyner, local hardware merchant, has written a novel with a Libya Hill background which the New York house of James Rodney and Company will publish this fall.

"When interviewed last night, the young author stated that his book was a romance of the Old South, centering about the history of a distinguished antebellum family of this region. The people of Libya Hill and environs will await the publication of this book with special interest, not only because many of them will remember the author, who was born and brought up here, but also because that stirring period of Old Catawba's past has never before been accorded its rightful place of honour in the annals of Southern literature.''

It makes George sheepish, angry and guilty.

When he returns to the city he is so oppressed by the imminence of publication that Esther fades into the background of his mind. Realising this, she asks him to a wonderful, a splendid party, perhaps with the hope that his love will return when he sees her in so gorgeous a setting. This is the most important narrative section of the book. The description of the day of the party, from morn till night, occupies perhaps forty thousand words, and contains remarkable portaits of Mr. Jack, Esther's maid Nora and the nymphomaniac, Amy Carleton. The party ends Wagnerianly, when fire breaks out in the apartment building where the Jacks live. A lift man dies in it; otherwise, there is no harm done. Esther and her guests are ravished with excitement and joy at the monstrous spectacle of flame and peril; and because George suddenly realises how different from his own is their attitude towards any disaster that does not affect them personally, he leaves Esther for ever. He has seen for himself at last that it is not possible for their worlds to touch.

In the autumn of 1929, two things happen: the great crash in the stock markets, and the publication of *Home to Our Mountains*.

"George Webber was just as confused and fearful as everybody else. If anything, he was more so, because, in addition to the general crisis, he was caught in a personal one as well. For at this very time he, too, had come to an end and a beginning. It was an end of love, though not of loving; a beginning of recognition, though not of fame. His book was published early in November, and that event, so eagerly awaited for so long, produced results quite different from any he had expected."

The campaign of vilification, of anonymous abuse, of sadistic and pietistic reproach directed against him by the people amongst whom he had spent his boyhood, terrifies and sickens him. Against the opinions of Libya Hill, the opinions of the professional critic count for little. He has reached a point in his life from which there will, indeed, be no turning back: Judge Bland had been only too right about that. For a while George is the subject of a New York lion hunt, pursued in the main by intellectual young women with some rather sordid motives for the chase. A kindly and sensitive letter from Randy Shepperton gives him a degree of comfort: and then the slump reaches Libya Hill, the bank fails, and Mayor Kennedy shoots himself. George, still behaving like a "wounded faun" about his book, is brought sharply to order by a visit from Randy Shepperton, who informs him that talk of *Home to Our Mountains* is drying up rapidly in the blistering wind of public disaster. Randy advises George to move away from Park Avenue and its associations; so George goes and digs himself into a Brooklyn basement, throwing up his instructorship and existing on what he has made out of his book. He lives in Brooklyn for four years, watching the daily round of the urban poor, the infernal existence between park bench, rubbish-dump and City Hall latrine of New York's submerged tenth.

During these years he is sustained, advised, controlled

by his editor Foxhall Edwards, of whom he makes a portrait mellowed by a teasing affection which upon occasion comes perilously near to skittishness; it has all the awkwardness of a public compliment paid in profound sincerity. Edwards is shown at home with his family, and the workings of his thought are explored by the means of giving it, as food, a newspaper cutting concerning an unidentified man who has fallen from the twelfth storey of a Brooklyn Hotel. Here Wolfe has used the method of free association—so free, in fact, that the reader senses a great deal more Wolfe than Edwards. Wolfe, when experimental, is never at his best.

George Webber is now beginning to meditate upon the subject of America, a monstrous land of confusions and terrors and marvellous promises. The thought of it obsesses him, and he decides that he must once more escape to Europe. In the summer of 1934 he comes to London, where he takes a room in Ebury Street. At this point Wolfe makes a study of what he believes to be a typical English charwoman. It is one of his least successful characterisations, underlaid with a tesselation of preconceived ideas: Daisy Purvis has the cosy, chivvying spirit of a Mother's Help and the self-respecting masochism of a butler, she aspirates words at random, she refers to the "Moddun Tempo" of life and she worships the Prince of Wales. She would be accepted as a charwoman on any West End stage by any audience of persons not in the habit of engaging their own domestics. She is, like most of Wolfe's English characters, stagey. She worships animals, is indifferent to human beings; is a flunkey towards the aristocracy, and has the outlook of a Tamurlaine towards the underprivileged. She expresses one of Wolfe's most fixed ideas where the English are concerned—that they are a people virtuous without, and brutish within.

In November the American novelist, Lloyd McHarg, comes to London. By mentioning George with enthusiasm in a newspaper interview, McHarg has stimulated a vast new interest in the young writer, and George is eager to meet him. (Sinclair Lewis helped Wolfe in a similar fashion, at a submerged stage in the latter's career.) To George Webber it seems that McHarg has the most desirable and lovely thing on earth, which is fame. The two men meet, enjoy a brief, frenzied, endurable intimacy and part again, leaving George older, colder and wiser. He knows now that the moment a man achieves fame, it becomes as nothing. It is a thing which, when grasped, turns to a handful of dust.

In 1936, feeling unable to face the publication of his second novel, George goes to Germany, where his first book has brought him already a considerable measure of recognition. Hitler has been in power for three years.

"Ever since 1933, when the change occurred, George had read, first with amazement, shock and doubt, then with despair and a leaden sinking of the heart, all the newspaper accounts of what was going on in Germany." He hopes now for reassurance, and at first finds those who will supply it. The airy and ordered vastness of the Olympic Games renews his faith in the peculiar genius of the German people, and the joy of being admired as "the great American epic writer", "the American Homer", gives him a temporary easing of the heart. Yet he cannot escape the sense of evil that is stifling his joy and making him afraid. It is the same evil he felt years before at the October Fair, but this time it is backed by the reality of the nervous hint, the whisper behind closed doors, the white-eyed, backward glance over the shoulder. Slow to believe any ill of the people and the country he so much loves, he is at last convinced by a frontier incident in which he becomes involved on his way back to France that Germany has indeed become terrible and corrupt.

The final part of the book consists of a long letter from George Webber to Foxhall Edwards, announcing and explaining the crystallisation of a philosophy. It remains a sketchy and spread philosophy, still with its vast lacunæ; but at least a stage has been reached from which there is unlikely to be any fundamental departure. In this letter George explains also, with prodigious circumlocution, why he has decided to break away from Edwards' literary tutelage. This is a thinly-disguised version of Wolfe's break with Scribner in the last year of his life.*

To Foxhall Edwards George suddenly makes a very strange confession. When he was at college in Old Catawba he and five other students, for a "rag", took a classmate out on to the playing-field one night, blind-folded him, and forced him to dance upon a barrel. The boy toppled over, fell on to a broken bottle neck, severed his jugular vein and bled to death within a few minutes. The "raggers" were expelled, brought up for trial, released in the custody of their parents, and deprived of civic rights. Citizenship was restored to them after three years, but news of the affair had spread throughout the state and the students were punished by public and appalling shame. A "dark and terrible imprint" was left upon all five young lives, and yet, as Randy Shepperton said on the night of the tragedy, had any of them been guilty of anything more than being damned fools? In

* See Appendix A.

F

the course of time Catawba people came to take this viewpoint, and even became sorry for the young men who had killed their fellow: "it cost a life, but it killed hazing in the state," was argued in their defence.

George tells Edwards that he is making this confession lest some day news of the affair should come to his friend's ears and he should put some wrongful construction upon it. George is anxious that Edwards should not refer his "radicalism"—in this case, his chip on the shoulder—to this cause. "Believe me, the Pine Rock case has nothing to do with it. It explains nothing. Rather, the natural assumption, for me as for the others who were involved in it, would be that the experience should have established me in a more staunch and regular conformity than I should otherwise have known."

The odd thing is this: that the college episode referred to in the letter to Foxhall Edwards did actually occur at the University of North Carolina, but it occurred before Wolfe's time and he had no connection with it whatsoever. It appears to have made a very profound impression upon him: but why did he attribute an active part in it to George Webber? Had he used it as one of the main psychological springs of the hero's life, understanding would be simple enough; but he explicitly states that it left no permanent scar, and explained nothing. It is just conceivably (this is pure speculation) a parable of the real, branding distress caused by the reception of *Look Homeward Angel* in Asheville, even as the breakaway from the guidance of Esther Jack is a parable of the breakaway from the literary "fathering" of Maxwell Perkins. The "accidental murder" was the "accidental" outraging of Wolfe's birthplace by the publication of the novel: the uproar in the state over the killing was the uproar in Asheville about the book: the forgiveness of the state, and the liberal-minded acceptance of the fact that the boys were not murderers but simply "damned fools", is the muting of local hostility towards Wolfe brought about by time, and by pride in his world acclaim.

Most probably the true explanation is other than this: but what it is, no one can ever know.

The letter and the book end with the most beautiful and electrifying poem Wolfe ever wrote. The poet has received annunciation of his imminent death. He turns to it not in distress and fear, but in peacefulness and joy, certain of immortality—"to a land more kind than home, more large than earth——"

"Whereon the pillars of this earth are founded, towards which the conscience of this world is tending —a wind is rising; and the rivers flow."

There is nothing to tell what gave Wolfe so sure a forewarning of his early death. It is just conceivable that the almost superhuman pressure under which he worked had made itself felt for some time past in the form of headache, mental exhaustion and spells of acute depression; but whatever truth there may be in speculation, the fact remains that this awareness set upon the last words of Wolfe's great novel the seal of that authority which is called genius. It is impossible to read the ending of this patched and sprawling work without a response not only from the brain and the heart, but actually from the flesh itself.

THE
FOUR
NOVELS

WOLFE's huge book of many parts defeats any water-tight analysis, for the whole matter is alive with shifting particles. The "Butcher" chapter in *The Web and the Rock* was originally in the manuscript of *Look Homeward Angel:* the second part of *The Web and the Rock*, which tells the Esther story, existed in manuscript before *Of Time and the River* was published, with the name "Eugene" standing for the name "George". It was then designed as a sequel to *Of Time and the River*, and was to be called by the title originally intended for the whole work, *The October Fair*. The story of Grover Gant's death and of his brush with a swindling shopkeeper, to be found in *The Hills Beyond*, have their place chronologically in *Look Homeward Angel*, but were written later. "The Microscopic Gentleman from Japan" (*You Can't Go Home Again*), Chapter 110 of *Of Time and the River*, and "I Have a Thing to Tell You" (*You Can't Go Home Again*) were all published separately in magazines. The novels are, in fact, so homogeneous in character that it would be possible to make the most arbitrary transfers of material from one book to the other without damage either to narrative or to mood.

Of Wolfe's work generally it is difficult to write with moderation, for the grandiose epithets persistently reiterated—"huge," "vast," "enormous," "fine," "rare,"—tend to transfer themselves automatically from the novels to the relevant criticism. They are his words, expressive of his own height, his own thought, his own conception of America. He hates what is "European and fancy,"—the dilettante, the æsthete, the precious, the writer for a clique, the tasteful natterer. His own influences are the Thunderers: Job, Ecclesiastes, Sophocles, Dante, Milton, Swift, Dostoievski, Joyce: he sees men huge and terrible and immortal.

He is a writer of stupendous egotism; his prime interest is in the development of himself as an artist and in his struggle to resolve his own mental conflicts. Because he naturally understands himself better than he understands anybody else, he assumes too much penetration on behalf of the reader; Eugene-George is only half the man. Wolfe omits many essentials concerning him simply because they are axiomatic to himself and therefore, he presumes, to everyone else. Eugene-George's life is one long bellow to keep his courage up. (It must be admitted that the ruse succeeds.) He yells of his triumphs with women because he is not so sure of himself as a lover; of his genius as an artist because he is not quite confident that any noise will be made about it elsewhere. Wolfe's height and Eugene's height is the source of a mania; it is the blessed compensation for the sense of personal inferiority. Look how huge I am! the hero cries, Look how much food, rich, gorgeous, ogreish food, I can cram into this giant frame! In *From Death to Morning* he attempts to disguise this pride by a curious essay on the plight of being too tall. Thomas-Eugene-George is given to this curious and clumsy form of covering-up. It is as if he had thought suddenly —I'm giving too much of myself away; I must fox them a bit. Thus the yelling and the bellowing, the bizarre exhibitions of masculinity, the denunciation and finally the disguising of the most cherished protective quality— tallness.

Wolfe is invariably more successful when his observer gives way to the observed. He knows Eugene-George completely, but is unable to tell more than the half of what he knows. Starwick, Elinor and Ann, the central characters in *Of Time and the River*, he knows only from observation, but his knowledge of them he is able to express *totally*.

By the side of Starwick, Eugene is no more than a woofing, tumbling St. Bernard. Starwick is a characterisation of genius; through him Wolfe amplifies one of his striking exit-lines in *Look Homeward Angel*:

"There is no place among the Boy Scouts for the androgyne—it must go to Parnassus."

(He concludes his chapters as firmly as Shakespeare concluding a scene with a couplet.) What we actually see of Frank Starwick is unprepossessing. At the university he is markedly "European and fancy"; he is a show-off, he patronises a cheap and nasty Italian restaurant and glorifies it in a ludicrous fashion, and he accepts quietly, as his due, homage to a genius he gives little practical evidence of possessing. His dress is dandyfied, his friendship erratic, his arrogance discomforting. In Paris, made wretched by his own homosexuality, he sponges off two women, one of whom (a monstrous creature, monumental as the succubus in Fuseli's *The Fireside*) takes her perpetual, abominable revenge upon him. Despite his fetich of delicacy and taste, he allows himself to be dragged round the *bas-fonds* of Paris by a doe-eyed, tight-waisted invert called Alec, who returns the wreckage in the morning in the most mannerly and smiling fashion. Eugene nevertheless assures us that Starwick is fine, marvellous, grand, swell: and though there is no factual evidence to support the contention, we implicitly believe him. Starwick *is* rare and wonderful, with a Renaissance fineness and flexibility. We are privileged to know him, to have even this slight insight into the marvel which is within him; and when Eugene, sick with rage and jealousy that big, dumb, beautiful Boston Ann should have set her own love upon this necessarily unrewarding object, knocks Starwick down at the corner of the Rue St. Honoré, we feel at once that Eugene is a great, hulking, insensitive male lummox who wants kicking. As his cruelty is aroused towards Starwick, so the reader's is aroused towards Eugene, who is, after all, despite his rawness, his stupidities, his lack of anything "fancy" whatsoever, implicitly the more valuable human being of the two.

The great passages in *Of Time and the River* are never the ones basically concerned with its hero. There are few things, either in *Look Homeward Angel* or *The Web and the Rock*, so fine as the really atrocious and most memorable incident that displays one of Elinor's most ingenious revenges.

Starwick has been out all night on a bout with Eugene, the two women and his new "great friend" Alec, whom he has picked up in a Montmartre bar. The women are unable to get him back to the hotel until four in the morning. By that time he is in a pitiable condition, blind and vomiting; it is not until six that he falls asleep. Elinor permits him to lie for a few minutes on the couch. She—

"regarded him for a while with an air at once contemplative and amused. 'And now,' she said cheerfully, 'to awaken the Sleeping Beauty from his nap.' She smiled her fine bright smile, but the lines about her mouth were grimly set and her eyes were hard."

A trip to Rheims has been planned for that day and she means him to make it, whether he likes it or not. The other girl, Ann, protests.

"Elinor smiled firmly and shook her head with a short, inflexible movement. 'No, sir,' she said quietly. 'Nothing is going to be put off. We are going to-day, as we planned. And Mr. Starwick is going with us! He may go willingly or against his will, he may be conscious or unconscious when he gets there, but alive or dead, he's going!' "

She is the Masterful Woman, the Punisher, speaking vulgarly because revenge is vulgar, and she wallows in it; it is the expression of her nostalgia for the therapeutic mud of retribution. The vengeance of the House of Dombey on Mr. Carker the Junior is a mild and humane rebuke, compared with the vengeance of Elinor upon Frank Starwick.

The nightmare journey by road is wonderfully and sickeningly described. When they get to Rheims cathedral Elinor insists on dragging Starwick from the car so that, supported on either side by the women, half-alive, his legs jellied beneath him, he may marvel at its beauties. Then they start on the return journey; from now on he is never wholly conscious, and at Soissons it seems almost as though he may die.

"After two ghastly hours in which they tried to revive him, persuade him to gird up his fainting limbs for the final effort, they got him back into the car. Ann covered him with blankets and held him to her for the remainder of the night, as a mother might hold her child."

They arrive back in Paris in the foggy, muffled dawn of the following day.

"They saw at morning, in the grey waking light, a waiter, his apron-ends tucked up, lifting racked chairs from the tables of a café, and on light mapled fronts of bars and shops the signs *Bière—Pâtisserie—Tabac*. Suddenly, the huge winged masses of the Louvre swept upon them, and it was grey light now, and Eugene heard Elinor's low, fervent 'Thank God'."

Only a teetotaller could fail to be shaken by the two chapters in which the story of Starwick's great drunk and Elinor's revenge is told. It is a monstrosity of cruelty. Elinor, the heavy, mature, authoritative woman, her face jolly and sardonic beneath the rather dowdy hat with the cockade, is one of the most remarkable of all Wolfe's characters. To know her is to be forced down into the abyss of human personality and to be tormented by the reminder of what is best forgotten, if life is to be in any degree pleasured and tolerable: which is, that the horror which shocks us in our own swift, private thought is founded upon truth, and that to the capacity for evil in men and women there is no end.

". . . The woman made no appeal at all to sensual desire: although she had left her husband and child to follow Starwick to France, and was thought by her own family to have become his mistress, it was impossible to imagine her in such a role. And for this reason, perhaps, there was something ugly, dark, and sinister in their relation, which Eugene felt strongly but could not define. He felt that Elinor was lacking in the attraction or desire of the sensual woman as Starwick seemed to be lacking in the lust of the sensual man, and there was therefore something in their relation that came from the dark, the murky swamp-fires of emotion, something poisonous, perverse and evil, and full of death.''

Even Esther Jack is a shadow beside her: and this is because Eugene retires in Elinor's presence, is only a figure in the background of her life, whereas in Esther's life Eugene-George is dominant always.

Of all the novels, *Look Homeward Angel* is the most tender, most personal, most hopeful. In it Wolfe writes of the two people to whom he gave the greater part of his love: his brothers Ben and Grover, who are called in the books by their real names.

Wolfe never married, and the sections of his work that deal closely with the love affairs of Eugene and Ann, George and Esther, are marked by a peculiar, almost ludicrous rhetorical violence. The bellowings, the howlings, the jeers, the rolling and abusive endearments seem to evidence some permanent and inalienable dissatisfaction. The "loss", the "search", are words that may often be narrowed, in Wolfe's writings, to a simple, personal reference: Eugene-George is searching for some ideal of love, some final sexual homecoming. Throughout the four novels there is not a single happy marriage. (There is no need to make an exception of the Foxhill Edwards ménage, since the chapter concerning it lies outside the book's real narrative.) Couples live in savage hostility, in bright-eyed, jovial enmity, in intolerable boredom and in mutual grey repulsion. Eugene even shrinks at his conception of the married life of the Leonards, both of whom he passionately admired. His vision of it is the queasy conjecture that comes to a child who has learned in some sudden and lewd fashion of the facts of birth and coition.

Of Ben and Grover, and indeed, of the entire Gant family, Wolfe writes with a kind of enslaved intimacy. To him, the family unit was the most powerful of all human groupings, which explains why the hostile reception of his first novel in Asheville affected him so profoundly. Ben, who is in the habit of making asides to his own invisible dark angel when exasperated beyond endurance by the bitter tomfooleries of Helen or his mother, is himself the guardian angel who broods over young Tom-Eugene, who gives him a watch to "keep time with" (—"and mind you keep it better than the rest of us have done"), who rages at Eliza when she sends the boy shabby to school or drives him out into the streets to "drum up business" for her boarding-house. The account of Ben's death from pneumonia is one of the most harrowing in the entire cycle.

Grover is the shy, gentle, incorruptible one. *The Hills Beyond* contains a striking sketch of him as a small boy, standing up to a swindling shopkeeper, and there is a further sketch which amplifies the account in *Look Homeward Angel* of his death, and of Helen's demand that Eugene shall come and see his brother "on the cooling table".

The central love affair in this novel, the one concerning Laura James, is treated as an idyll; Eugene has not yet reached that stage of bogus sophistication and cherished self-disgust which urges him to address Ann as "you great big, dumb, beautiful, Boston bitch".

It was a bad thing psychologically that Wolfe eventually made the effort to drive Eugene Gant out of his system. With George Webber grew the hatreds and revenges born out of frustration, out of the enormous, heart-cracking, preposterous effort to set down in writing not merely a shadow of his thought and his experience but the whole of it. With Webber, the humour grew more harsh, the venom more personal. *The Hills Beyond* contains a most enjoyable, most vicious *Portrait of a Literary Critic*, which should endear Wolfe particularly to fellow-writers because he says, in his angry, grinning fashion, what the other novelists would like to say and for business reasons don't dare. "Sheer elfin genius!" whinnies the revolting Dr. Turner, while his wife smiles secretly at the young author as if she knew something absurd about him that he didn't know himself, meanwhile murmuring that he is like an elf—yes, an elf! But all the same, this is a far cry from the Wolfe of the early, comic *pastiches;* the personal hate has entered in, and the dry rot of disappointment.

In his foreword to the English edition of *The Web and the Rock* J. B. Priestley claims that this is the best of Wolfe's novels, the most varied and most massive of all. "Massive," yes—even more compound than the others of all the giant key-words (train, city, root, ship, lost) and witch-words (yell, howl, bellow, gold, burble, ropey); but varied, no. It is, of the four long novels, the most egotistical. In *Look Homeward Angel* Eugene was concerned to reflect the Gants, especially Oliver, Eliza, Helen and Ben: in *Of Time and the River* to reflect Starwick, Elinor and Ann. They were persons in the limelight of Eugene's observation, he himself standing outside the circle of radiance. But in *The Web and the Rock*, Eugene-George is the entire play. We see Esther only as he saw her, through his dark and distorted mirror, and can catch only the most fleeting glimpse of her reality.

The idea of Esther Jack comes in the concluding chapter of *Of Time and the River*. Eugene is returning, more knowledgeable, not very much wiser, to America from Europe. On the ship he sees a woman with whom he instantly falls in love, once and forever. She has a "rosy face burning with the excitement of the voyage"; she is "somewhat deaf"; in "her tone, her manner, her indignation" there is something "irresistibly comic". She is little; she has a "small, flushed flower" of a face. She is Jewish. Her surname we are not told, but her first name is Esther.

In *The Web and the Rock* she appears as the thirty-five-year-old mistress of George Josiah Webber, the young man from Catawba, ten years her junior. She is a wealthy woman, a theatrical designer of great talent. She has a "very fresh, ruddy, and healthy face . . ." a "small, rosy, and good-humoured face". She can be self-appreciative and comic. She is a "flushed, rosy and excited little person". She has the hair of all the women with whom Eugene-George is in love—the hair of Ann, of Margaret Leonard, coarse brown hair touched lightly with grey. She is, in fact, the woman Eugene Gant met on the home-going ship.

Like Eugene, George Webber has studied literature at the university, has walked in the burning and mysterious city, has taught English to the listless and the eager, and has sown wild oats in Europe. Like Eugene he is hysteric, intemperate, passionate, destructive, and tortured by the sense of being *lost*—which is the word upon which all the novels are founded. And, like Eugene, he falls in love with Esther Jack.

What Wolfe has done is to project Esther (the same woman, recognisable) into another novel about the same young man, who now bears a different name: yet there can be no doubt that it is to the Esthers of the world (the patron-mistresses who worship, succour, establish and devour) that Eugene would naturally have turned after the fading-out of his hopeless love for Ann. Ann was still a girl, would be a girl always. Esther has always been a woman.

The reason for this transposition, not merely of a heroine from one book to another, from one life to another, but of the same hero into a new name and a new flesh, was this. Wolfe had planned to follow *Of Time and the River* with a new cycle of Eugene's development, which was to be called *The October Fair*. Three factors caused him to change his mind. The first was the unhappiness and embarrassment *Look Homeward Angel* had given his family, and the painful memory of his own reaction to the howls and abusings of Altamont's corner-boys and parish Savonarolas. The second was the realisation that there was so much in his childhood which he had forgotten to record. There would be no place for flashbacks in subsequent Gant books: the only solution open to him was the creation of a new character. Thirdly, he now felt that he had evolved a more objective attitude towards himself and his work. Writing to Edward Aswell, the Harper's editor, shortly before his death he said he had come to loathe the name "Eugene Gant"; the type of characterisation had come to typify for him "a kind of romantic self-justification". He now proposed to write a book "of discovery, of union with life; not a book of personal revolt, hence of separation from life!".

Yet the "new" character evolved by Wolfe was not helpful to this idea of spiritual shift. He lopped a foot from Eugene's height, lengthened his torso, shrunk his legs; made him nearly a grotesque, but not quite. He rounded upon him and blackened him; left him his monstrous, ogreish love-talk but dwindled him down with an infusion of anti-Semitism, spite and brutishness. George speaks now with the tongue of Eugene and of devils; but he is still the same man, and the romantic self-justification clings around him still, only it is less explicit. Wolfe created George Webber not because he was growing closer to men and women, was seeing them with a greater objectivity, but because, without realising it, he was drawing away from them.

Nebraska Crane, the Cherokee boy, George's childhood friend, is drawn magnificently, out of love. He is not an autobiographical character. He was created, Aswell suggests, not because he was the friend Wolfe had known in boyhood, but because he was the friend Wolfe always longed to have known.

In *The Web and the Rock* Nebraska Crane is presented by means of a bright, rough crayon drawing, and is not fully developed until, in *You Can't Go Home Again*, he rings George up during the wretched period of home-town abuse to comfort him with his unalterable friendship and with his enthusiastic delight in the fact that he himself has not been left out of the book. He is indeed a boy's dream of a friend, the one who cannot hurt because he is utterly without evil. He is the protector, who drives the bullies away with a threat to kill them if they molest young George again, and who really means it, who would break their heads without a doubt. He is the famous baseball player unspoiled by the adoration of young men and children, who will sign an autograph for anyone, and smile, and make a joke about it also. He is the symbol of permanent loyalty, certain as the rising of the sun. He is goodness itself, the only character that George Webber has observed without interposing the smoked glass of his own torments. Otherwise it is the *lack* of objectivity, not any increase in that quality, which cuts *The Web and the Rock* so sharply away from the Gant books and even, though in a much lesser degree, away from *You Can't Go Home Again*.

Just as Proust's novel contains two entirely "good" characters, Marcel's mother and grandmother, by whom the moral stature of all the other characters is measured, so Wolfe's novel presents as his key to absolute human sanity and goodness of heart the baseball hero Nebraska Crane. He is the only person in the two novels, *The Web and the Rock* and *You Can't Go Home Again*, by whom Wolfe's charity is unneeded: there is simply nothing ill to say of him.

Esther Jack, far more important to the narrative, infinitely more developed as a characterisation, is not one half so vivid; and this is because, while George is content to stand aside and observe Nebraska, he has given Esther the role of holding the lamp that shines down upon himself. She is there for his benefit, and not he for hers.

She offers her whole life to the naif, bombastic, verbose and frequently detestable young man for two reasons: she loves him, and she believes he has genius. And she offers it in the full knowledge of what she is doing, in the full realisation that she will be destroyed. Wolfe's treatment of this wild, exalted and fundamentally ugly love-affair is curious. More than any other writer of three decades he expresses the turmoil that exists in America. He worships America; she is the expression of his own being, his own unresolvable conflicts. More than any other writer, he holds her essence within himself. Her brutality he symbolises by his own; her vulgarity is the vulgarity he fosters and cherishes within himself. For Eugene-George expresses himself, when in love, in a manner reminiscent of a drunken business man at a national Realtor's Conference in Kansas City. He "howls", "bellows," "yells," "breathes stertorously." His mania for food gives a cannibalistic slant to his love-making. " 'Steak, hey?' " he cries, when Esther lures him back to her temporarily with a reminder of her perfect cooking, " 'I'll steak you!' He does so. 'Pot roast, hey? Why you—*you're* my pot roast!' "

And again, in an earlier scene:

"Deliberately he would step forward again, bending over her; then, tentatively, he would take her arm and pull it gently like a wing.

" 'Shall it be a wing?' he would say. 'A tender wing done nicely with a little parsley and a butter sauce? Or shall it be the sweet meat of a haunch done to a juicy turn?'

" '*Und ganz im Butter gekocht*,' she cried, with a merry face.

" '*Ganz im besten Butter gekocht*,' he said . . . 'Or shall it be the lean meat of the rib?' he continued in a moment, 'or the ripe melons that go ding-dong in April?' he cried exultantly, 'or shall it be a delicate morsel now of women's fingers? . . . O you damned, delectable, little plum-skinned trollop! . . . I will eat you like honey, you sweet little hussy!' "

The long, repetitive account of George's life with Esther holds a sadistic, adolescent pleasure. He treats her abominably; she admires him tenaciously. Sometimes she is moved to cry out, "Oh, you are mad! . . . And your mind is black and twisted with its evil! ''—but in the end he has to push her out by the shoulders, as she will never leave him voluntarily.

Now the odd thing in Wolfe's handling of the affair is this: that while he allows George's self-pity to be clearly apparent, he does not succeed in making the right effect with it. Usually, self-pity on the hero's part does one of two things to the reader: either it forces his own reluctant, rueful sympathy, or it makes him contemptuous. George's self-pity is merely baffling. As Mr. Priestley remarks, ''. . . He (Wolfe) is apt to indulge himself, like a tipsy undergraduate at the end of a long evening, in long passages of a vague and bogus profundity, as if announcing, but at great length, that there is a 'something somewhere if we could only find it'.'' The fact is that George does strike us as three-quarters bogus—as Eugene also strikes us, *when he is left entirely alone upon the stage*. It is impossible to believe that this was the effect Wolfe wished to produce. Eugene-George is the reflection of himself; the three novels are, as we understand the word, and in face of the author's disclaimers, autobiographical to a high degree—and Wolfe was never a judge of what was bogus in his own writing.

Wolfe's conception of George Webber was almost certainly different from the one received by the reader. The physical description of Webber, made out of a desire to destroy Eugene Gant, is a blunder. The impression given is that the hero is not merely unhandsome but downright hideous; it is extraordinarily difficult to see what *immediate* charm he could have had for Esther Jack (he must have had it, or she would not have responded to his first letter) and entirely baffling to find her, at the end of *The Web and the Rock*, maundering to a policeman of Webber's "wild beauty". The reader feels that no love could be purblind as this. Any writer of fiction will have experienced the difficulty of disguising physically a living person whom he wishes to put into a novel; the moment he has changed the large man into a small one, made his hair fair instead of dark, his eyes brown instead of blue, the original personality has disappeared with the original physical attributes. Wolfe wrote of George Webber as an ugly man, short-necked, barrel-chested, simian—

> ". . . The effect of this inordinate length of arms and hands, which dangled almost to the knees, together with the stooped and heavy shoulders and the out-thrust head, was to give his whole figure a somewhat prowling and half-crouching posture"—

but as he wrote, it was himself whom he saw. It is this division in Wolfe's mind that makes for puzzlement in the reader's.

Not only is the body wrong for this "new" hero, the family history is wrong also, for it bears no relation to the development of his character. Wolfe explains with extreme care the position of young George Webber, tainted in the eyes of his uncle and aunt by the sin of his father: yet there is no indication whatsoever in the record of his adult life that he would have been one whit different had the circumstances of his youth been the same as Eugene Gant's. The story of Webber's childhood is finely told, but it has nothing to do with the rest of the narrative and is really no more than an arbitrary interpolation between two cycles of the hero's life.

The only real difference between Eugene and George, apart from the physical, is that George is the older and more disillusioned man of the two. George would have seen through Starwick in five minutes, and pitied him only with difficulty; whereas Eugene saw in him a culture that was shapely, esoteric and desirable, George would have seen only the "European and fancy". The attitude, actual and potential, towards Francis Starwick may serve as a touchstone for the two nearly similar natures.

The most attractive woman of the four novels is Ann, in *Of Time and the River*, who, though Wolfe dealt with her almost as a subsidiary character, the Maria to Elinor's Lady Teazle, emerges in the full warmth of humanity. Esther Jack is too brilliant to touch the heart, too adroit, too self-reliant, too little in need of chivalry. Ann is locked in the "incommunicable prison" of herself, a big girl, sullen-faced, slow of words, no hand at witty conversation: but she is full of goodness, and when she smiles she is radiant and beautiful. She is the type of woman to make a success of nursing, her tenderness expressed not in words but in a gruff practicality. Also, she is precisely the woman to fasten her love forever upon some utterly unresponsive object. She is perfectly "right" for Eugene, counterbalancing his wildness with her stability, his wordiness with her silence, his passions with her stillness; the tragedy is that she has already abandoned her hope of happiness, and has nothing to offer any man, whether "right" for her, or wrong. She moves Eugene to a torment of love and pity.

". . . And he kept mumbling thickly, 'Christ! Christ! What a pity! What a shame!' not knowing what he was saying, conscious only, with a kind of sickening horror, of the evil mischance which had with such a cruel and deliberate perversity set their lives awry, and of the horrible waste and loss which had warped forever this grand and fertile creature's life and which now would bring all her strength, her love, the noble integrity of her spirit, to barren sterile nothing."

She is the most beautiful of all Wolfe's women because she is the most vulnerable. Laura James has refuge in her own essential selfishness, Esther Jack in the social shell, delicate as spun glass, hard as a diamond, which has grown about her. Neither will be forever lost, as Ann is lost, neither will ever be without some manner of refuge.

It is interesting to see how Wolfe's opinions of other writers were reflected in his own endeavour. His attention was always upon the "great event", love or death, or slump or war, that affected *everyone*. He had no use for what he believed to be side-issues—that is, matters affecting only a limited group of people. He wrote to Mrs. Roberts:—

> "During the most inventive and mature years of his genius G. B. S. expended his great powers of satire on the one thing he thought worthy of drama—the thesis——
>
> "Then a war comes along that kills twenty million people and destroys nations and suddenly we can't convince ourselves that *Mrs. Warren's Profession* and *Widowers' Houses* deal with the biggest things in the world after all. If I were Shaw now, I think I should feel as if I had been equipped with a mighty bludgeon but had spent my life braining gnats."*

Wolfe, who was always trying to make his books swallow the whole of life, could not understand why Shaw dealt, play by play, with certain aspects of it only. To him, the themes of *Mrs. Warren's Profession* and *Widowers' Houses* were isolates; he could not relate them

* *Atlantic Monthly*, December, 1946.

to the mechanism of society, in which every cog has its function in the whole machine. It is impossible to imagine Wolfe devoting a book to child neglect, slum clearance, or prison reform. He attempted to write always of matters that were of general application.

For Eugene O'Neill he had a tremendous admiration, but was afraid the playwright was developing a "backward tendency" towards the primitive. O'Neill had shown this tendency in *The Emperor Jones;* the new play, *The Hairy Ape*, was to show a stoker on a liner retrogressing steadily towards the condition of primitive man. To Wolfe, with his spread and flaring visions of the future, this was a dangerous and an evil thing, philosophically and artistically.

"Tragedy, if continued in this vein, will become sordid and brutal . . . Great tragedy, I think, must look ahead."*

This is the true voice of the young man who, in the square of Altamont, decisively rejected the authority of the dead.

Molnar's *Liliom* interested Wolfe because the play took a new turn of interest *after* the hero's suicide. This, again, appealed to Wolfe's forward-looking, and his refusal to believe in any real ending. While Liliom is dying the hardened police officers drag the body away, all the while talking about their jobs, the new wage scale, the mosquitoes, and any other topic of the moment. While Ben lies dead Horse Hines achieves the peak of mortician's artistry from which he will progress to new triumphs. While Ann fades into the eternal fogs of her own doomed and idiotic life, Eugene sets eyes upon the eager and rosy face of Esther Jack.

* *Atlantic Monthly*, December, 1946.

Wells' *Undying Fire* pleased Wolfe.

"This is one of the few moderns I have had time for, but rarely have I been more stimulated. He's not a profound man, but he's a very sound man . . . a living proof of the benefits of a broad and intensive education to the training of a first-class mind."*

Despite the backhanded flavour of this praise, Wells did appeal to him as the reverse side of the medal. Wells' gruff commonsense complements Wolfe's philosophical woolliness: Wells' astringent prose Wolfe's sensuous rhetoric: Wells' sense of a pathway Wolfe's sense of loss.

Of the four novels, *Look Homeward Angel* is the most complete, but *Of Time and the River* the finest. The latter has an honesty of youth that subsequently became obscured by the writer's unrealised desire to appear more mature than he really was. Wolfe's perception of human nature was adult, and so were the scope of his vision and the scale of his achievement; but his outlook was a boy's outlook, and George Webber at twenty-five is only Eugene Gant at twenty, but scowling more, in an attempt to appear more ruthless and more disillusioned. The four books together make one masterpiece and cannot correctly be judged as works separate one from the other; it is enough to suggest that with *Of Time and the River* Wolfe reached his early summer, and that the two subsequent novels represent the fall of his brief year.

* *Atlantic Monthly*, December, 1946.

THE
PHILOSOPHY

ASHEVILLE was a small provincial town. Wolfe, son of a lower middle-class family, respectable, but compelled at all times to live meagrely, had in embryo many of the adverse tendencies such an environment frequently breeds—anti-semitism, colour-prejudice, xenophobia, feeling of inferiority—and they kept pushing upwards; but he had the virility and breadth of imagination to drive them down again. The saving force was his natural optimism and his belief in the grandeur of mankind, but this was an optimism in conflict with an instinct to despair, a faith in conflict with an instinct to condemn. The purest expression of Wolfe's optimism is to be found in Eugene Gant: of his conflict, in George Webber.

George Webber is anti-semitic, coarse-minded in an adolescent fashion (he speaks of his casual adventures with women always in terms of "going with whores") and attracted emotionally to the kind of Germanic earthiness which, distorted, ends up in the rites of Wotan-worship, the eugenic theories of the Deutschesmädelsbund, and the forcing of elderly Jews to clean out latrines without swabs or rubber gloves. Indeed, on his first visit to Germany, he feels himself for the first time in his life "found".

And yet one is somehow assured that this distortion, this ultimate twisting of the spirit, will never take place. Unlike Henry Miller, Wolfe does not accept the Spenglerian metaphysic. American writers are peculiarly addicted to summarising concretely their motives and artistic intentions in the body of their work. In *Tropic of Cancer* Henry Miller explains himself as follows:

"It may be that we are doomed, that there is no hope for us, *any of us;* but if that is so then let us set up a last agonising, blood-curdling howl, a screech of defiance, a war-whoop! Away with lamentations! Away with elegies and dirges! Away with biographies and histories, and libraries and museums! Let the dead bury the dead. Let us living ones dance about the rim of the crater, a last, expiring dance. But a dance!"

This pronouncement is equated, in a rather less cheerful fashion, by Spengler:

"Only dreamers believe there is a way out. Optimism is cowardice. We are born into this time and must bravely follow the path to the destined end. There is no other way. Our duty is to hold on to the last position, without hope, without rescue."

Wolfe's philosophy has nothing in common with all this. He is not tormented by a sense of doom, but rather by the fear that he may never be able to set down in words the immortal grandeur of America, of mankind, *of himself as a living creature*. He sings the Body Electric as raucously as Whitman: and if he lacks Whitman's vaguely suspect optimism, it is because he desires to do more, to go further, than Whitman ever contemplated. The root of his distressful and frantic seeking is not a fear that all things are nearing their end and that time is too short for him to grasp them before they melt away; the root of it is his conviction that the splendour and culture of a whole nation is yet only in its infancy, and that he may not live long enough to see it in the full glory of its youth. And it is not only the good that seems to him magical; he realises always that the dark is as much a part of him as the light.

The later sections of *You Can't Go Home Again*, which deal with George Webber's second visit to Germany in the spring of 1936, gives an insight into Wolfe's political ideas, so far as he had made any clear formulation himself.

George goes to Berlin, where he finds himself moderately famous. His book has had good sales in Germany, and German critics have written about it with enthusiasm. The chestnut trees are in full bloom, the café terraces are full of people, and "always, through the golden sparkle of the days, there was a sound of music in the air". It is the time of the Olympic Games, and George observes how nobly the organising power of the great German people is displayed. Yet he has begun to sense something ominous behind the cleanly blare, the glitter, the beauty of Order. Some of his German friends speak to him of certain matters in a circumlocutory fashion, and behind locked doors: others are too afraid for speech.

"He did not see any of the ugly things they whispered about. He did not see anyone beaten. He did not see anyone imprisoned, or put to death. He did not see any men in concentration camps. He did not see openly anywhere the physical manifestation of a brutal and compulsive force."

It is an interesting fact that some of the most haunting and repulsive stories of local Nazi pogroms appeared in the American magazine *Life* almost immediately after Hitler came to power. Apparently George read them; it is curious that they made so little impression. He comes to

Berlin three years later with the unsophisticated attitude of the tourist who cannot believe anything can be wrong with a country where the streets are swept and the trains run to time. In *The Web and the Rock*, George speaks with passionate, ironic fury about the lynchings of the South. In 1936 he is so far from crediting the lynchings of Fascism that he has to arrive at his final conclusions by means of stray hints, backward glances, domestic atmospherics. It is only at the last, when the train is halted on the frontiers of France and Germany and a fellow-traveller, a terrified, money-smuggling Jew, is caught by the German police, that he comes to an assessment of belief.*

"The experiences of that final summer in Germany had a profound effect upon George Webber. He had come face to face with something old and genuinely evil in the spirit of man which he had never known before, and it shook his inner world to its foundations. Not that it produced a sudden revolution in his way of thinking. For years his conception of the world and of his own place in it had been gradually changing, and the German adventure merely brought this process to its climax. It threw into sharp relief many other related phenomena which George had observed in the whole temper of the times, and it made plain to him, once and for all, the dangers that lurk in those latent atavistic urges which man has inherited from his dark past. Hitlerism, he saw, was a recrudescence of an old barbarism. . . ."

He believes this barbarism, the "primitive spirit of greed and lust and force," to have been always the true enemy of mankind.

* See Appendix B.

"It took on many disguises, many labels. Hitler, Mussolini, Stalin—each had his own name for it."

George's political views are based upon emotions rather than economics, are sensory rather than scientific. He uses the words "greed", "lust," "force" as abstractions: not asking "greed—for what?" "lust—for what?" "force—to what end?" Politically, he is rather like the White Queen: he can believe six impossible things before breakfast. But if politics without science are dangerous, politics without heart are as much so. Wolfe, essentially a humanist, felt rather than analysed the trend of the future.

Of the spirit of greed, lust and force he continues:

". . . America had it too, in various forms. For wherever ruthless men conspire together for their own ends, wherever the rule of dog-eat-dog is dominant, there it is bred."

He feared for the immediate future of his country, was confident of her ultimate emergence into an orderliness based upon justice, and upon happiness pursued and captured.

George Webber, sitting the night through in the darkened rooms of German friends, behind the bolted and shuttered windows, is only now able to make some manner of synthesis.

"So it was, in this far place and under these profoundly moving and disturbing alien circumstances, that I realised fully, for the first time, how sick America was, and saw, too, that the ailment was akin to Germany's—a dread world-sickness of the soul. One of my German friends, Franz Heilig, later told me this same thing. In Germany it was hopeless: it had already gone too far to be checked now by any measures short of death, destruction and total ruin. But in America, it seemed to me, it was not mortal, not incurable—not yet. It was desperate, and would become more desperate still if in America, as in Germany, men became afraid to look into the face of fear itself, to probe behind it, to see what caused it, and then to speak the truth about it. America was young, America was still the New World of mankind's hope, America was not like this old and worn-out Europe which seethed and festered with a thousand deep and uncorrected ancient maladies. America was still resilient, still responsive to a cure—if only—if only men could somehow cease to be afraid of truth. For the plain and searching light of truth, which had here, in Germany, been darkened to extinction, was the remedy, the only one, that could cleanse and heal the suffering soul of man."

He makes his final statement of philosophy in the long letter to "Foxhall Edwards" (Maxwell Perkins) with which his life's work ends.

"Your own philosophy has led you to accept the order of things as they are because you have no hope of changing them; and if you could change them, you feel that any other order would be just as bad. In everlasting terms—those of eternity—you and the Preacher may be right: for there is no greater wisdom than the wisdom of Ecclesiastes, no acceptance finally so true as the stern fatalism of the rock. Man was born to live, to suffer, and to die, and what befalls him is a tragic lot. There is no denying this in the final end. *But we must, dear Fox, deny it all along the way.*"

Thomas-George believes that to conquer and destroy the "enemies" (fear, hatred, slavery, poverty and need), nothing less than the complete revision of the existing structure of society will suffice: though he gives no idea by what means this is to be achieved. The evils he hates can only be met by Truth:

"With the courage of the truth within us, we shall meet the enemy as they come to us, and they *shall* be ours. And if, once having conquered them, new enemies approach, we shall meet them from that point, from there proceed. In the affirmation of that fact, the continuance of that unceasing war, is man's religion and his living faith."

This is a long way from Spengler, but it is as far from the Oxford Group. It is not a personal philosophy, nor is it a philosophy for bringing about, by means of hearty, honest smiles, a reconciliation between capital and labour. It has a little in common with Bunyan, more with Blake. It is, in fact, the philosophy of a man of good will, stout heart and small political sense who says: "I want to be good!—And I can be, if I try. And you can. And so, together, we must be."

Wolfe recognised the evils of society and was filled with noble rage and disgust by the inhumanity of man to man; but his essential idealism prevented him from perceiving the causes of social disease or from accepting any positive theory as to a means by which the cure might be sought. In a sense he is a symbol of America herself, reflecting more nearly than any other writer of his time the state of mind of a great country faced suddenly with political and economic crisis—a vast country of tremendous potential for social, industrial and cultural expansion, baffled by problems that appear to be without connecting link. Trends of supreme importance flow strongly, but to no convergence. Great industrial progress keeps pace with great depressions; the highest standard of living in the world glitters above a hard stratum of appalling poverty; the unquestionably great contribution of America to the history of democracy, through the War of Independence and the Civil War, is balanced by a history of repression to which the existing labour laws, the fear-ridden life of the Southern negro and the memory of the Sacco and Vanzetti case bear abundant witness.

More Englishmen understand England, more Frenchmen France, more Russians Russia, than Americans their own country: in America patriotism appears to be more mingled with bewilderment than in any other land in the world. Wolfe loved his country with a peculiar and moving personal force and believed in her superb and golden future; but of her complex social and economic structure he had only the vaguest and most troubled of ideas.

He could never, by his nature, have been a politician; his view of men is too near-sighted for that. He sees a character as if he stood breast to breast with him, their faces almost touching; men are to him so huge, so oppressive in their closeness to himself that he is never able to comprehend the forces which move them, and which they themselves move. It is because of this inability to understand anything related to the structure, social and economic, of society, that at the end he railed against a world which appeared to be none the better for his brief lifetime of railings:

"... the world's fool-bigotry, fool-ignorance, fool-cowardice, fool-faddism, fool-mockery, fool-stylism, and fool-hatred for anyone who was not corrupted, beaten and a fool."

Yet this is not the cry of the dissident, the politically

disillusioned; it is the cry of the boy who was never any good at arithmetic.

If Wolfe has nothing in common with Spengler or with Miller, neither has he with Koestler or Céline. He is not anarchistic any more than were the Elizabethans, with their prodigious and chaotic curiosity. He does not desire the eternal search; he passionately desires a solution. Not to be lost—to be found. The enormity, the richness, the squalor, the beauty and the locked and costive meanness within America tear him to the heart. He is looking for some sort of equation. He dreads the answer, for the very agony of the questioning holds the sum of wonder and beauty; but he cannot rest until that answer is discovered:

"I believe that we are lost here in America, but I believe that we shall be found . . . I think that the true discovery of America is before us. I think the true fulfilment of our spirit, of our people, of our mighty and immortal land, is yet to come."

All his life he was given to saying nothing nobly; but always in the faith that even an abstract nobility was better than no nobility at all, that it was at least a shout of affirmation on the side of the angels. It was not in his nature to contribute more than this to the eternal cerebral struggle to discover for mankind a good manner of living.

His incapacity for practical political thought gave him a horror of being nudged into any direct political action. "What to do?" he wrote to Mrs. Roberts, on April 6th, 1938. . . . .

"Like you, I have become in the last few years tremendously involved with the state of the world— as my consciousness of life has enlarged, my consciousness of self has dwindled; there are things now that so afflict me in the state of man that I think I would take up arms against them, or give my life to stop them—but what to do?"*

People urged him, he protested in his tone of angry apology, to sign his name to petitions for this or for that cause—on behalf of the Spanish Republic, the share-croppers in the South, Tom Mooney, the "Scottsboro' boys"; what should he do about all this?

"The observation of Voltaire in *Candide* that at the end of all the best thing is for a man to tend his garden used to seem cynically and selfishly callous to me, but I am not so sure now that it does not contain much deep wisdom and much humanity as well. Perhaps the best thing that a man can do is just to do the work he is able to do, and for which he is best fitted, as well as he can. And perhaps his greatest service to other men can be rendered in such a way as this."*

Perhaps. Yet underlying this conclusion is this drag of Wolfe's fear that once he became involved in any political movement, he would be caught by the obliga-tions of political discipline. He was, he continued, feverishly, always being badgered by worthy people to take sides or make proclamations. Many writers and leagues of writers seemed to be tied up in all this sort of thing, and while he "admired their energy", and did not question their sincerity, how on earth did they find time to get their own work done? "One does not write books by carrying placards in front of the French Consulate, or having interviews with President Roosevelt."*

These explanations to Mrs. Roberts have the dull ring

* *Atlantic Monthly*, February, 1947.

of self-justification in the face of buried doubt. Doubtless he had no time to picket consulates or talk to the President: yet he could surely have found one second in which to append a signature had he wished to do so.

". . . I think I would take up arms against them, or give my life to stop them. . . ."*

The truth is that by the spring of 1938 Wolfe was in full political retreat even from those vague points reached by implication. He did not admire for their energy the writers engaged in political controversy; he dreaded them. They were a threat to his passionate isolation, an isolation all the more intense and all the more comprehensible because of his unique obsession with the flight of time. He really did have a sense of being engaged with Time in a struggle to the death. A symbolic painting might have shown him desperately scrawling away down the length of an interminable papyrus while Time, an enormous eagle, ripped with her beak at parchment and pen, and flapped her wings about his head to blind him. From this struggle he could allow nothing to deflect him, not even the nag of his own social conscience. He was engaged in cultivating, "at the end of all," not a garden, but the desert of an entire continent.

Above all things Wolfe is a humanist: he would have hated the shy, sly, delicate novels in to-day's fashion, of which the action may lie in any country one cares to fancy, of which the people bear careful, middling names that might belong to the nomenclature of any race, and express thoughts that summarise the common mean. He postulates always a certain country, a certain man: thickens his pages not with symbols, or with types, but with huge and terrifying and adorable human beings.

* *Atlantic Monthly*, February, 1947.

Wolfe was always, entirely, boy and artist—never, like Proust, man of the world, Dreyfusard (or an equivalent), etymologist, dilettante of military science; never, like Joyce, runaway Catholic, scientist, expert on water-taps. He knew the blind agony of his personal world and of the world about him, and he showed these worlds to themselves; and he died angry and sorrowful that neither had taken the directive he had been unable to give.

THE
AMERICAN
RICH

WOLFE's attitude towards the rich of America is defined with fair coherence in three separate sections of the whole work. The first is the Joel Pierce episode in *Of Time and the River*, the second is the quarrel with Esther Jack in *The Web and the Rock*, and the third is the semi-symbolic outbreak of fire following the Jack party in *You Can't Go Home Again*.

Eugene, a hard-up English instructor working in his spare time at the writing of some ambitious but highly derivative plays, meets again an old university friend, the rich Joel Pierce. Joel, an exceedingly nice fellow who wears his wealth as easily as a man might wear an old raincoat, insists that Eugene shall come and stay at his lovely and fabulous home on the Hudson river. The Pierces, despite the awful authoritarianism and narrowness of the older members of the family, cannot help but command Eugene's hungry admiration, which is voracious spiritually and physically. His whole attitude towards them is symbolised in his meditation before the ice-box, a meditation full of desire for the physical sating of his great body, æsthetic sating of his great, fuddled mind. It adores, and it sneers.

"I think—now let me see—h'm, now!—well, perhaps I'll have a slice or two of that pink Austrian ham that smells so sweet and pungent and looks so pretty and delicate there in the crisp garlands of the parsley leaf!—and yes, perhaps, I'll have a slice of this roast beef, as well—h'm now!—yes, I think that's what I'm going to do—say a slice of red rare meat there at the centre—ah-h! there you are! yes, that's the stuff, that does quite nicely, thank you—with just a trifle of that crisp brown crackling there to oil the lips and make its passage easy, and a little of that cold but brown and, oh!—most—brawny gravy—and, yes, sir! I think I *will*, now that it occurs to me, a slice of that plump chicken—some white meat, thank you, at the breast—ah, there it is!—how sweetly doth the noble fowl submit to the swift and keen persuasion of the knife—and now, perhaps, just for our diet's healthy balance, a spoonful of those lima beans, as gay as April and as sweet as butter, a tomato slice or two, a speared forkful of those thin-sliced cucumbers—ah! what a delicate and toothsome pickle they do make—what sorcerer invented them—a little corn perhaps, a bottle of this milk, a pound of butter and that crusty loaf of bread—and even this moon-haunted wilderness were paradise enow—with just a snack,—a snack a snack——"

Before the richness of the Pierce icebox, the Pierce library, he is lost in adoration and loathing. He cuts himself free of Joel not so much because his pride will not permit him to accept what he cannot return, but because he despises the rich for not appreciating what they have. In his heart, he rages at them because they are fools. He spends his last night at the Pierce home in the great library.

"They were all there, from thundering Æschylus to the sweet small voice of perfect-singing Herrick, from grand plain Homer to poignant Catullus, from acid and tart-humoured Horace, from the lusty, vulgar and sweet-singing voice of Geoffrey Chaucer, the great bronze ring and clangorous sonority of John Dryden, to the massy gold, the choked-in richness, the haunting fall and faery of John Keats. . . ."

He knows that these pure voices have chanted unheard in the vast room in which he sits, and he hates the rich for their smiling deafness.

"So did that great treasure of unread, purchased, and forgotten books speak to him in the silent watches of the night, as they stood there, lonely, small and bought, on a rich man's shelf."

In the morning, when he says good-bye to the sensitive and lovable Joel, the farewell is final. Both of them know it. Eugene breaks off his friendship with the Pierces not because they have, by divine right of their wealth, all the things he might consider due to himself by his own divine right of genius; but because their minds are too small to know their own luck.

This is a youthful impression, accurate enough so far as it goes, but incomplete. Eugene-George has not yet spent those four years in Brooklyn which are to add to his dislike of the American Rich another element. At present he finds them shallow, unappreciative and Philistine; he has not yet come to look upon them as callous to the bone.

With Esther Jack and her circle the matter is somewhat different. Here is artistic society, not fabulously rich, as the Pierces' is rich, but wealthy enough. Mr. Jack, the *mari complaisant*, the good-natured, successful business man, does not ask his wife questions.

"He was not a man to rip the sheets in darkness or beat his knuckles raw against a wall. He would not madden furiously in the envenomed passages of night, nor would he ever be carried smashed and bloody from the stews. A woman's ways were no doubt hard to bear, but love's bitter mystery had broken no bones for Mr. Jack, and, so far as he was concerned, it could not murder sleep the way an injudicious wiener schnitzel could, or that young Gentile fool, drunk again, probably, ringing the telephone at one a.m. to ask to speak to Esther."

Therefore, his wife is able to lead her own hard-working and delightful life in the theatre, and to adore, cosset and cook for young George Webber in her quiet "work-place", which is the entire top floor of an old four-storey house on Waverly Place.

The arrangement is, of course, ideal, and George should have found it so: but after the first raptures he does not. Upon the days of joy and of artistic creation his black "moods" intrude, growing violent even to the verge of insanity. Though he loves Esther, he treats her at times with a disgusting brutality which is half bullying and half a whine. He loves her because she is poised, brilliant, successful, of exquisite good taste; and he hates her for all these things. He rages constantly against her friends, who are assured and noted people. What he loathes here is the dilettantism of the successful, the amateurism of the established. To him it is intolerable that they, the "arrived", the noted, the confident, the flexible, should be of such slight, sleazy stuff compared with himself, the beginner, the outsider, the blunderer, the unpublished.

Yet even in the midst of these hatreds he falls from faith in himself—one of those awful, desolate plummet falls so destructive, so rotting in their terror, yet without which Thomas-Eugene-George would have been immeasurably poorer as man and as artist.

"And suddenly he saw himself as a member of the whole vast shabby army he despised: the pale, futile yearners of the arts, the obscure and sensitive youths who thought their souls too fine, their feelings too delicate and subtle, their talents too rare and exquisite for the coarse and vulgar apprehension of the earth."

He wonders now whether he himself is not brother to the pitiful, aspiring members of his literature class who sneer at the success they so longingly desire for themselves, and which they will never attain.

He cannot be sure: and so his attitude where Esther's circle is concerned is more suspect than it is towards Joel's. He hates the writers, artists, actors, because they, with one hundredth of his genius, have arrived at their destination while he is still upon his long and sweating journey. He is not yet mature enough to solace himself with the thought that their destination may merely have been Long Island; while his is Mars. He hates the rich, slack-living Park Avenue women not because they are "Jews", "whores" (his anti-semitism spurts out of him in a defensive stream like ink from the cuttlefish) but because the women he could afford for himself back in Catawba were only squalid drabs living in the stench and dirt of Niggertown. He has a masochistic impulse to relate these adventures to Esther.

". . . And inside the house, it was always hot and close and smelled of shiny furniture and horse-hair and varnish and strong antiseptics. And you could hear a door that opened and shut quietly, and someone going out. One time there were two of them who were sitting cross-legged on a bed and playing cards.

And when I left they grinned and showed their toothless gums at me and called me 'son'."

So far, the element of personal jealousy is active; and indeed, it is never wholly eradicated. It expresses itself also in his curious attitude towards the English tradition —an attitude compounded of contempt and admiration. Eugene, living in Oxford, transcribes the English accent stagily and with huge malice; but when he makes the rounds of the public-houses his great longing is for the Proctor to mistake him for a student, and to order him out. It is a considerable sorrow to him that this never happens.

At the time of the first quarrel with Esther, George does not hate the rich because they are the owners of millions of lives. He does not hate them because they no longer serve even so useful a rôle as patrons of the artist. He hates them chiefly because their money can buy them these things: beauty of person (clean, sweet hair, smooth skin, fragrance of body, brightness of eye, a prolongation of youth—compare a rich woman of forty with a working-class woman of the same age, then see if the former does not look the younger of the pair by a decade) and beautiful things to possess, fondle, and forget to dust. He wishes to destroy the hegemony of wealth, not because the poor would be the less poor for its destruction, but because the wealthy are knaves and fools, unworthy of so great a curacy. So far as economics are concerned George Webber is entirely naif, seeing the aches, rheums and cancers of the world only in terms of the humours of his own body.

In *The Web and the Rock* George makes what he believes to be a final break with Esther and goes to Europe. "Fleeing from a love that still pursued him, he had become

a wanderer in strange countries. He had travelled
through England, France and Germany, had seen
countless new sights and people and—cursing, whoring,
drinking, brawling his way across the continent—had
had his head bashed in, some teeth knocked out, and his
nose broken in a beer-hall fight." (This is Wolfe on
his high horse, and at his most truculent.)

Lying in a hospital bed in Munich, George Webber
feels at last at peace with himself. He has not, by his
own admission, learned much—learned little more, in
fact, than that you can't have your cake and eat it; but
the more roaring and hysteric nonsense has been driven
out of him and he decides that he must now go home to
Esther.

They take up their lives together very much as they
left off, though now he has refused to return to the house
on Waverly Place but has insisted that she share two
rooms which are his own. His first book has been
accepted by publishers of standing, and he is looking
forward with excitement and apprehension to its coming
out. He is happier than he has ever been in his life.
When, however, the first startling pleasure of realising
that he is indeed a professional writer has worn off and
he has returned to his old teaching job, he becomes
aware that Esther is no longer in the forefront of his mind.

"She was aware of this and resented it, as women
always do. Perhaps that's why she invited him to the
party, believing that in such a setting she would
seem more desirable to him and that thus she could
recapture the major share of his attention. At any
rate, she did invite him. It was to be an elaborate
affair. Her family and all her richest and most brilliant
friends were to be there, and she begged him to come."

George at first refuses, but is badgered into acceptance. The day set for the party is the one exactly a week before that crash in the New York stock markets which brought an age to an end.

The Jacks live on the tenth floor of a solid, handsome, neat but not gaudy apartment house. The big room, prepared for the party, might strike a stranger as "not only homelike in its comfortable simplicity, but even, on closer inspection, a trifle shabby". There are books on three of the walls, extending a third of the way up them, books to be read, and bearing the reassuring marks of reading. Crackling pinelogs throw their radiance from the great marble hearth. There is something, Esther thinks, " 'sort of grand—and simple about it all.' And indeed" (George comments) "there was. The amount of simplicity that could be purchased even in those times for a yearly rental of fifteen thousand dollars was quite considerable."

This is, in fact, the home of the highly sophisticated Rich, a miracle of the best very delicately disguised as the consoling commonplace.

George Webber shambles sourly into the party to find a glittering company assembled: distinguished men, beautiful women, writers, publishers, actors. There is a notorious slut, there is a wife patiently and civilly enduring the company of her husband's mistress. The talk is loving and fine and brilliant, the food magnificent to taste and most glorious to behold. Piggy Logan comes and gives his marionette show just as the fun starts to flag a little, but has no great success. Then, as the guests are wondering what to do next, fire breaks out in the building. Mr. Jack marshals guests and servants together and after a few delicious terrors the party descends to safety by the service elevator, the other being out of order.

It is a splendid show for all; Esther's face flames with excitement. Crowds gather in the courtyard of the building, persons in every stage of dress and undress mill together in a scene that might have been produced "by the combining genius of a Shakespeare or a Breughel". The spectacle is fantastic.

"Before very long the wisps increased to clouds, and suddenly a great billowing puff of oily black smoke burst through the open window, accompanied by a dancing cloud of sparks. At this the whole crowd drew in its collective breath in a sharp intake of excitement—the strange, wild joy that people always feel when they see fire.

". . . Mrs. Jack gazed upwards with a rapt and fascinated expression. She turned to Hook with one hand raised and lightly clenched against her breast, and whispered slowly—

" 'Steve—isn't it the strangest—the most——?' She did not finish. With her eyes full of the deep sense of wonder that she was trying to convey, she just stood with her hand loosely clenched and looked at him."

It is the most wonderful unrehearsed party-trick imaginable, and all Mrs. Jack's guests are disappointed when the fire is at last brought under control and they are able to return to the apartment. Esther, always jolly and warm to those who serve her, asks the doorman what has happened to the elevator man, and receives an evasive, rather brusque answer. She is rebuffed, almost angry; in fact, she makes an irritable comment to her friends. It has never occurred to her that the fire has been other than a show, a *grand finale*, never occurred to her that someone might have died in it. For example, the missing elevator man.

George realises now that his life with Esther has come to an end. The new element in his hatred of the American Rich has appeared: he has seen that there must be a vaster world than this Christmas-tree planet of wealth, jewelled and starred and sparkling.

"He had seen it naked with its guards down. He had sensed how the hollow pyramid of a false social structure had been erected and sustained upon a base of common mankind's blood and sweat and agony . . . And that was where Esther and this world of hers came in. In America, of all places, there could be no honest compromise with special privilege. Privilege and truth could not lie down together."

Just before this summary of George's conclusions there is a brilliant touch, one of Wolfe's most perceptive, most sober and most felicitous. Esther, always quick to sense what is in her lover's mind, *knows* what he is thinking, and knows that they are conversing now at the end of their journey. Without the slightest change in her manner, the least hint of her fear, she makes one final attempt to hold him: by pretending that she has, throughout that evening, been of his own heart and mind, looking with his own contempt at those who can look upon the tragedy of others only as an entertainment for themselves —or, more precisely, who can conceive of there being no unhappiness for others, so long as they themselves are happy. She scarcely puts this pretence into words, speaking not of herself and her own guests, but of the strangers who swarmed into the court. It is beautifully done; but it is too late, and it cuts no ice with George

Webber. He leaves her behind in the world one concrete conclusion has caused him to reject, and she fades forever from his story.

George Webber was made "confused and fearful" by the slump. He saw it almost in the light of a poetic disaster, something descending from a furious Heaven like Noah's flood or the doom of Sodom. Only two italicised pages are devoted to it directly,* though its effect upon the people of Altamont-Libya Hill and its indirect effect upon George Webber (Libya Hill stopped talking about his scandalous novel when the Citizens Trust Company failed and Major Kennedy blew his brains out) is carefully studied. George compares America in 1929 with the cicada, which, in the last stage of its life-cycle, emerges from the earth looking more like a fattish grubworm than a winged insect. It then climbs the bark of a tree and hangs by its front legs. Suddenly the outer skin splits down the cicada's back and a new creature comes forth. This remains motionless in the sun until the body begins to quiver with life, the iridescent wings bud and grow, and at last the new cicada flashes off, "a new-born thing released into a new element." From this idea Wolfe builds an exquisite and optimistic analogy, but indicates no precise magic whereby the glorious and looked-for qualitative change may be expected to come about.

Wolfe could feel the impact of eternal events without being able to analyse them. The atmosphere of the Slump is here, the "false calm and desperate anxiety".

* It must be noted here that the italicised passages linking the narrative of *You Can't Go Home Again* were pieced together by Edward Aswell from what he could find in Wolfe's writings, and from what he remembered Wolfe to have said. Therefore, though this idea of the cicada was obviously Wolfe's own, it is safer not to ascribe these passages to him too closely.

"Security was gone, and there was a sense of dread
and ominous foreboding in the air."
Nevertheless, it is impossible to escape the impression
that he hurried over the world catastrophe and returned
with relief to the personal life of George Webber, nor is
it surprising that this should have been so. At the time
of writing *You Can't Go Home Again* the effects of the
crash were still being felt, even by those who had
escaped any immediate consequences. It was hard even
for the political writer to achieve a perspective, and for
a writer like Wolfe it would have been a hopeless task.

The next advance in the social consciousness of George
Webber is his first encounter with the urban poor, the
destitute of the city of New York. Disgusted by Park
Avenue, he rushes characteristically to the other extreme
and goes to write in a basement in Brooklyn. With the
money made by his book he has paid his debts and has
now given up his teaching job. He is dependent from
now on solely upon his literary earnings.

Every night, at one o'clock or later, he walks across
Brooklyn Bridge and with a "horrible fascination" visits
the public latrine of New York City Hall. Here he finds
the dregs of the homeless men, huddling and fighting for
a little warmth and shelter.

"Some were those shambling hulks that one sees
everywhere, in Paris as well as New York, in good
times as well as bad—old men, all rags and bags and
long white hair and bushy beards stained dirty yellow,
wearing tattered overcoats in the cavernous pockets of
which they carefully stored away all the little rubbish
they lived on and spent their days collecting in the
streets—crusts of bread, old bones with rancid shreds
of meat still clinging to them, and dozens of cigarette

butts. Some were the 'stumble bums' from the Bowery, criminal, fumed with drink or drugs, or half insane with 'smoke'. But most of them were just flotsam of the general ruin of the time—honest, decent, middle-aged men with faces seamed by toil and want, and young men, many of them mere boys in their teens, with thick, unkempt hair. These were the wanderers from town to town, the riders of freight trains, the thumbers of rides on highways, the up-rooted, unwanted male population of America. They drifted across the land and gathered in the big cities when winter came, hungry, defeated, empty, hopeless, restless, driven by they knew not what, always on the move, looking everywhere for work, for the bare crumbs to support their miserable lives, and finding neither work nor crumbs. Here in New York, to this obscene meeting place, these derelicts came, drawn into a common stew of rest and warmth and a little surcease from their desperation.

"George had never before witnessed anything to equal the indignity and sheer animal horror of the scene. There was even a kind of devil's comedy in the sight of all these filthy men squatting upon those open, doorless stools. Arguments and savage disputes and fights would sometimes break out among them over the possession of these stools, which all of them wanted more for rest than for necessity. The sight was revolting, disgusting, enough to render a man forever speechless with very pity."

After talking a little with these derelicts he goes out into Manhattan, considers the Woolworth Building, the "silvery spires and needles" of Wall Street, and rages at the blind injustice of it all. The City Hall latrine has a profound effect upon Wolfe's imagination; it appears again in the "Letter to Foxhall Edwards", as the symbol of all that is lost and foul and sad. His is young man's socialism, based on the generous rage, the infuriated, baffled pity; like the majority of young, middle-class intellectuals, he looks for "the people" in the doss-house and upon the benches of the midnight parks. Wolfe's hero, the typical man of extremes, the psycho-pathic rebel, never makes contact with any sort of organised labour; for him, the protagonists of the conflict are, on the one hand, Mr. Jack, and on the other the half-starved, rotting vagrant crouching in the latrine by Brooklyn Bridge.

THE
INCOMMUNICABLE
PRISON

"LIKE a tipsy undergraduate . . . announcing . . . that there is a 'something somewhere if we can only find it'" Wolfe certainly was: but with this difference, that his search for the "something somewhere" continued into sobriety, and never ceased. However vain a quest, it was not an ignoble one. Wolfe experienced more often than most people that flash of light just beyond the edge of vision which is accompanied by the conviction that "the whole thing is there", if only one could turn one's head quickly enough to catch it. He knew the sensation of a single supreme idea nearly formulated, then lost forever; an idea which, once crystallised, would be sufficient to change and irradiate the entire thought of the world. The experience is not unlike a sudden, violent and inexplicable thirst. He knew that we are imprisoned in the shell of our flesh, and that we cannot speak the words which would set us free; that mankind is hopelessly inarticulate, able to record in speech only the most broken chart of his thought.

"Could I make tongue say more than tongue could utter! Could I make brain grasp more than brain could think!"

All his life Wolfe tried to do this impossible thing, and in trying burned himself out. His entire work is a forcing process. With every word he wrote he was trying to say more than any human being had ever said

[124]

of the marvel of the earth and of man. He wanted to capture in words the experience of *nearly understanding:* and, more preposterous and more wonderful, to be the first man in all the world to understand completely. This was the ideal by which he lived and by which he laboured, an unsophisticated, incorrupt and terrifying ideal. A child might have conceived it, as a child might simply have conceived the desire to be, some day, the greatest man that ever lived.

"The deepest search in life, it seemed to me, the thing that in one way or another was central to all living, was man's search for a father, not merely the father of his flesh, not merely the lost father of his youth, but the image of a strength and wisdom external to his need and superior to his hunger, to which the belief and power of his own life could be united."

Yet all Wolfe succeeded in producing was a history of violent endeavour. At the end he knew his questions were yet unanswered, and that he had come no nearer to the "something somewhere" than he had been in the days when he was writing his one-act plays. Proust, who would never have contemplated an odyssey such as Wolfe's, came infinitely nearer to achieving Wolfe's desire. The incidents of the dipped madeleine and of the stumble at the unexpected step are both transcriptions of an intense and familiar human experience: as no man before him he caught it, analysed it, and related it to the past. Proust, seeking to explain the personal miracles that are rooted in time past, and Wolfe, seeking to explain the personal miracles which he feels must be leaning down to him from stems that are rooted in the future, were working to opposite ends, yet Proust, in his deadly patience, penetrated further into the incommunicable prison than Wolfe in his gigantic fury.

When Wolfe died his work was done. It is all there, ended as surely as a work of music is ended by the last downward cut of the baton. Had he lived, he would have gone on writing: but becoming always more confused as he faced a second world war that must have set him in hopeless conflict with himself.

It is no accident that *Look Homeward Angel* is the most clear-sighted of his novels. Born into the lower middle class life of a small mountain town, he pictured the familiar world with an objectivity altogether remarkable. The farther he journeyed from Asheville the more baffled he became, and the less sure of himself. When he left the mountains he discovered that he could not go home again, and for the rest of his life was haunted by the sense of being a wanderer, and adrift. He was lost in the city and in the foreign lands; in 1929 the whole world of his most intimate experience came to an end, and he never came to terms with the new one. In his loneliness he was America herself, America of the Nineteen Twenties, huge, young, aggressive, unfound, like an adolescent at a grown-up party, and he looked with desire and awe upon the future. He managed to "greet the future with a cheer," proclaiming his certainties, thundering his reassurances: but he was never again as confident of himself as Eugene had been when he spoke with Ben's ghost beside the stone angel.

With all his gigantic faults, his prolixity, his ranting, his stupefying absurdities, Wolfe is incomparably the most significant figure in three decades of American literature. His egotism arises from a profound desire to analyse the nature of his own being, not from a passion to display himself to others. He is the egotist uncon-

scious of an audience. Hemingway, for all his sophistication, his taste, his superb selectivity, always gives an
impression of being aware that company is present, and
that he is responsible for its entertainment. He is
permanently on his mettle, eyes and ears sharpened, alert
for the least sign of weariness or irritation. Wolfe is
labouring upon a mental excavation that engages his
entire attention; he would no sooner make a concession
to an interruptor than a surgeon would break off in the
middle of trepanning to look out of the window at a
Salvation Army band.

He never acquired "poise". His later work displays
even more sharply than his earlier books the defiance
that comes of being uncertain. His antagonism towards
modern European culture sprang from worshipful envy
of its long ancestry. By his reference to "fancy" writing,
he means the over-sophisticated writing of the intellectual who believes fundamentally that his learning has
made him superior to the common man; and this is a
peculiarly European outlook. Wolfe felt that the
foundations of an American literature were still being
laid; and he therefore resented the writer whose ease
arises out of a conviction that he is simply continuing,
and adorning, a tradition. The youthfulness of his
country weighed heavily upon Wolfe; he thought of
America *culturally* as the brilliant but underprivileged
Board School boy matched against the University Man
of Europe—a boy who, because of his very disadvantages,
must work twice as hard and succeed three times as
brilliantly.

He never acquired "professionalism". He never
learned to trim his work, polish it, or play safe with it.
He was never able to make himself comfortable at

literary parties. He wrote because he wished to communicate something that seemed to him inexpressibly urgent; nothing else mattered. This is why his books carry so powerful a sense of his personality; they are the most intimate writings, the most naked and the most trustful, of this generation. He set out in search of an impossible ideal—to communicate that which is incommunicable. He ended with a philosophy that is little more than a few vague conclusions and a few verifications. What he did achieve was a finished portrait of the artist as a young man, and within this man the portrait of a continent. "The whole thing's there—it really *is*."

The artist is a small-town boy of remarkable physical and mental attributes, and the ambition of a Cæsar. The niggling life of home drives him into a frenzy of revolt; he thrashes about like a whale, striking wildly at everyone and everything, yet holding in reserve that one last element of bitterness which might make retreat impossible. Struggle as he may against the family unit, he is forever bound to it. His head is giddy with the riches of a vast reading, and his daydreams are created out of literature rather than by any observation of romantic love at close quarters—in fact he has seen none, and the marriages of Altamont freeze him to the bone. When ambition takes him to the city, he is inhibited by the consciousness of his own provincialism. He is Ulysses without a ha'porth of faith in Penelope, contemptuous of her and of her smart friends. The world outside America defeats him because he believes in the power of kinship above all things, and is most tied by it; and when a people to whom he considers himself kin* passes into a state of corruption, he is thrown into bewilderment and despair. Politically

* The German people.

(so far as he is political at all) he might have veered towards a romantic fascism, if it were not that he is basically objective and absolutely *kind*.

Socially he is unreliable, the guest whose problematical behaviour fills the prospective hostess with apprehension. A fancied slight will move him to sullenness or to insult. Though he gets drunk in the grand manner he is really a poor drinker, and a small amount of alcohol will unbalance him. Among women he searches for a mother, and when he finds one, and has been mothered to satiety, he breaks free of her loving with signal violence. He believes himself harsh and self-reliant. In fact, he cares deeply for what people say of him. He resents the whimsical, the sly, the "delicate", as a boy resents some "girlish" gift or occupation.

(Oddly enough, Wolfe greatly admired Sir J. M. Barrie.

"I think Barrie is the most significant dramatist in the English-speaking world to-day because he really is carrying on the great tradition of our drama. This is an arch-heresy here where some of my young critical friends consider him 'sentimental'. Is it not strange how the academic, critical point of view shrinks nervously away from the sympathetic? I have never read a play of Barrie's that didn't give me this curious 'mixed' feeling. He is not trying to 'prove' anything (thank Heaven) but like Shakespeare and other old fogies, is more interested in the stories of human beings than in the labour problem. That's why I believe his plays will outlast those of his contemporaries, because people at all times can understand and appreciate the emotion of other people."*

* Letter to Mrs. Roberts: *Atlantic Monthly*, December, 1946.

This feeling for Barrie consorts queerly with Wolfe's outbreaks against the "elfin" touch; it is possible that his admiration for Barrie's fine technical qualities blurred his perception of the philosophy behind the plays. Logically, Peter Pannishness should have infuriated him, because though Wolfe longed to break out of boyhood into full maturity he could never quite achieve the transition; while Peter Pan actually wishes to remain in the irresponsible and subordinate state of being a child.)

The artist is oppressed by the limitations, not only of his own powers of verbal expression, but of any man's. He longs for the gift of tongues, that he may make all things clear to the whole of the world. He believes in the existence of absolute goodness and absolute evil— in everything, in fact, that seems to him large and plain and incontrovertible. He believes that the best thing to do in face of darkness and doubt is to state a creed at the top of the voice, and then trust to luck. The cicada America, sloughing off her dead shell, would emerge beautiful and new into the dazzling air of morning.

"I believe that we are lost here in America, but I believe we shall be found."

"Man was born to live, to suffer, and to die, and what befalls him is a tragic lot. There is no denying this in the final end. *But we must, dear Fox, deny it all along the way.*"

Believe: that is the only word the prisoner has discovered after his life sentence in the cell of flesh. Had he for one moment entertained the slightest hope of success it would be a confession of failure, but he knew, before he died, that the search had been an end in itself.

The most striking feature of the Gant-Webber novels

is their youthfulness. They do, indeed, look outward upon the future as a boy looks out in fear and terrifying hope upon his manhood. Their sincerity is a boy's sincerity, and their confidence is that friendliness which is offered to all men only before experience has brought commonsense and distrust, balance and corruption.

When *Look Homeward Angel* was first published in England, it was the young people who greeted it with excitement and with that curious uprush of personal affection which upon rare occasion greets the author of a novel that has come upon certain hidden springs in the wilderness of the reader's desire. Young men and women between seventeen and twenty-three years of age felt that in some obscure way Wolfe was their spokesman; perhaps, after all, he had managed to send out some message from the incommunicable prison. His lyricism was the expression of their own longing to put into words the wonder and strangeness of coming out of childhood. The Laura James idyll which, to the mature critic, shows Wolfe at his weakest, to the adolescent represented love as he most deeply wished to find it. The boy who felt himself in any way restrained or subjected by his parents was moved by Eugene's protest to his family after the fight with Luke and Ben: this, thought the boy, is what *I* should like to have said, if only I could have found the words. The optimism towards the future, *despite the gainsaying of a dead man*, encouraged the young reader to feel himself Promethean, capable of defying not only those set in authority over him by reason of kinship, age and experience, but of defying also the supernatural authority—God, and the voice of the Prophets. Wolfe gave to the young man a conviction that whatever might be the defeat of others, his own future would be straight and shining as the path of the sun across the sea.

In his lifetime Thomas Wolfe made an international reputation. A great deal of critical attention has been devoted to his work in America and in Germany also, but already the colours of his fame are beginning very slightly to dull. In a sense England and America have still to discover him. He has his place with Hemingway, Faulkner and Steinbeck in the histories of American literature; but only as one modern writer among others. His comparative importance is as yet unassessed.

Beside him Faulkner seems neurotic and obscure, Hemingway over-sophisticated and Steinbeck, a novelist of power and solidity, to have a certain recessive quality, as if his people and his places were set a little way back from the full light of the reader's vision. Faulkner's "Southness", so much deeper than Wolfe's, perverts his vision like a black scarf tied over one eye. Though he lacks Wolfe's ear for words and indulges in bouts of word-juggling that not infrequently degenerate into nonsense, he is the more mature writer of the two; but he lacks Wolfe's humanity and affectionate understanding of ordinary people. Steinbeck, an expert craftsman who has achieved a mature philosophy and has something vital to say, sees humanity rather than human beings. No Steinbeck character is completely an individual, but typifies a group. Because of this, the force of the message itself is weakened; we always believe something a friend tells us first-hand rather than something we read in the newspapers, and what Tom Joad has to say would have gripped the attention even more straitly if Joad had been a man we could have recognised instantly (not only as a type but as a single human being) had we met him on the street. Wolfe, who is infinitely less ordered a thinker than Steinbeck and with far less of real importance to communicate, never drew a character who was not visible even to the lines in the palm of the hand, whose voice was not audible even to the lowest mutter of speech, whose behaviour in any set of circumstances could not be anticipated with certainty to the last gesture.

Faulkner, Steinbeck and Hemingway, despite their powerful consciousness not merely of adding to, but of building, a national culture, could easily have been Europeans. They look upon Europe with a sympathy unclouded by the jealousy or sense of "inferiority" that was ineradicable in Wolfe. They are, in fact, grown-up, while he remains rooted in adolescence. In spite of his prejudices, Wolfe brings to Europe a curiously sharp understanding, though this tends to embrace the colours, scents and weathers, the whole "feel" of a country, rather than its people. He views the English nervously, the French with a degree of contempt, and speaks warmly of the Germans alone.

He is American as Whitman was American: and like Whitman realises the *earliness* of the time at which he speaks. Although he cannot claim, as Whitman could, to be among the pioneers, he does believe himself in the company of those who follow after them to develop the ore and oil of a new continent. His tremendous pride, the pride that vented itself in hostility towards the friends of Esther Jack, towards the English, and towards the publishers "Rawng and Wright", is counteracted by an even greater joy in being young, in being uncertain, of sitting down with the primer and learning the world from the beginning as once he learned new languages.

[133]

Alone among the writers of his generation he understands that the indigenous culture of his country to-day is as young as England's was when Chaucer struck open the great way of modern English letters, and that the spaces of her future are unbounded.

APPENDIX
A

Look Homeward Angel and *Of Time and the River* were published in the United States by Scribner. In the last year of his life Wolfe changed his publisher and took a manuscript of over a million words to Harper, who published it as two novels, *The Web and the Rock* and *You Can't Go Home Again*.

The reason for Wolfe's defection from Scribner was this. The Scribner editor, Maxwell Perkins, had done an inestimable service to Wolfe in helping him to order the vast mass of his work, to control it and to draw it together. Certain literary circles in America began to whisper, with staggering absurdity, that Perkins had helped him to write his books. This whisper preyed on Wolfe's mind. Almost any other writer would have been able to shrug this nonsense off, but not he. He had to prove to the world that he was indeed the "onlie begetter" of his own books, and, more important, to prove to himself the baselessness of his growing terror that in the malicious gossip there might have been a grain of truth. Had he, in fact (he asked himself), in any way been influenced by Perkins' advice?

He prefaced the work that he took to Harper with a statement which is inacceptable to many critics. The new book—"marked not only a turning away from the books I have written in the past, but a genuine spiritual and artistic change. It is the most objective novel I have ever written."

To the end Wolfe remained on terms of close personal friendship with Perkins, whom he appointed his literary executor. The reasons that had prompted Wolfe's "disloyalty" were fully understood by both the publishers concerned, and Harper continued to publish his work in format originated by Scribner.

A full and fascinating account of the whole incident is to be found in the Scribner Centenary publication, *Of Making Many Books*, by Roger Burlingame (1946), from which I have taken the foregoing details.

APPENDIX
B

Wolfe, who had some German blood in him, was strongly and romantically Germanophile. He visited Germany in 1935 prepared to believe the best, but his own honesty would not let him carry such a belief too far. He wrote in a long letter that the German people were— "the cleanest, the kindest, warmest-hearted, and the most honourable people I have met in Europe"; and when he commented upon the ugly aspects of Nazism which (probably through his friendship with Ambassador Dodd and his daughter Martha) were impinging upon his reluctant consciousness, the words have a defiant ring: ". . . . This evil is so curiously and inextricably woven into a kind of wonderful hope which flourishes and inspires millions of people who are themselves, as I have told you, certainly not evil, but one of the most childlike, kindly and susceptible people in the world."

Nevertheless, a story published in the *New Republic* three years later, *I Have a Thing to Tell You*, shows how greatly Wolfe's understanding of the "fatal and destructive thing" (Hitler Fascism) had deepened. This story was incorporated, with certain changes, in *You Can't Go Home Again*, and tells of the Jew whose escape from Germany is thwarted by the police. Wolfe turns in murderous fury about the symbol of Hitlerism, the fat and shaven officer who arrests the Jew. It is his reaction from the years of struggling to misunderstand. He has understood now: but rather late.

Yet Germany was still the "dark lost Helen"—

". . . the dark lost Helen I had found, it was the dark found Helen I had lost—and now I knew, as I had never known before, the countless measure of my loss —the countless measure of my gain—the way that would now be forever closed to me—the way of exile and of no return—and another way that I had found. For I knew that I was 'out'. And that I had now found my way."

For this matter and quotations I am indebted as before, to Roger Burlingame's *Of Making Many Books*.